Buying a Small Business With Little or No Capital

A PRACTICAL GUIDE WITH $0-DOWN STRATEGIES

Rudy LeCorps

All Rights Reserved. Copyright © 2002 Rudy LeCorps

No part of this book may be reproduced or transmitted in any form or by any means, graphic, electronic, or mechanical, including photocopying, recording, taping or by any information storage or retrieval system, without the permission in writing from the Publisher.

Published by RGL Learning

For information, please contact:

RGL Learning
30 Constitution Way – Unit 104
Jersey City, NJ 07305
http://rgllearning.com
ISBN: 0-9744156-0-X

Printed in the United States of America

To all the dedicated people who made this tutorial workbook possible

TABLE OF CONTENTS

LIST OF TABLES 11

PREFACE 13

ACKNOWLEDGEMENTS 16

INTRODUCTION 17
    BUYING VS. STARTING 17

DECIDING ON A BUSINESS TO PURCHASE 24
    CHOOSING AN INDUSTRY 24
    RESEARCHING AN INDUSTRY 29

FINDING A BUSINESS TO PURCHASE 32
    ACQUISITION SEARCH 32
    NEWSPAPER 34

BUSINESS BROKERS	35
THE INTERNET	38
CONTACTING BUSINESS OWNERS DIRECTLY	41
DIRECT MARKETING AND NEWSPAPER ADVERTISING	43
TRACKING LEADS	48

DETERMINING THE CONDITION OF A BUSINESS. 50

DUE DILIGENCE	50

DETERMINING THE PRICE TO PAY FOR A BUSINESS ... 72

VALUATION ANALYSIS	72
WORKING WITH THE FINANCIAL STATEMENTS	78
ADDITIONAL VALUATION TIPS	89
VALUING INTANGIBLE ASSETS	90
PROFESSIONAL PRACTICE VALUATION	91
FINAL NOTE ABOUT VALUATION AND PREMIUMS PAYMENTS	92

FINDING MONEY TO PAY FOR THE BUSINESS ... 98

RAISING FINANCING & $0-DOWN STRATEGIES	98
SPECIAL FINANCING SECTION: AN UNCONVENTIONAL SOURCE OF CAPITAL	121

LEGAL AND TAX ISSUES ... 127

ACQUISITION OPTIONS	127

RUNNING THE BUSINESS ... 130

HIRING AND KEEPING GOOD EMPLOYEES	131
MANAGING BUSINESS FINANCES	133

EPILOGUE ... 139

ABOUT RGL LEARNING ... 141

ABOUT RUDY LECORPS 142

APPENDIX & ADDITIONAL RESOURCES AND CASE STUDY 143
    NO-MONEY-DOWN ACQUISITION CASE STUDY 143
    VALUATION RESOURCES ON THE INTERNET 149
    SKELETON BUSINESS PLAN 150
    SAMPLE EXECUTIVE SUMMARY 152

GLOSSARY 163

BIBLIOGRAPHY 173

INDEX 176

SIGN-UP FOR THE PUBLISHER'S FREE ONLINE COURSE 188

List Of Tables

TABLE 1 TABLE OF INDUSTRIES 26
TABLE 2 INDUSTRY QUALIFYING TABLE 31
TABLE 3 SAMPLE BROKER SPECIFICATION SHEET 36
TABLE 4 WEB SITES LISTING BUSINESSES THAT ARE FOR SALE 39
TABLE 5 SAMPLE LEAD TRACKING SHEET............................. 49
TABLE 6 SAMPLE LETTER OF INTENT (I)................................ 51
TABLE 7 SAMPLE LETTER OF INTENT (II) 56
TABLE 8 DUE DILIGENCE TABLE I 63
TABLE 9 DUE DILIGENCE TABLE II... 67
TABLE 10 VALUATION DOCUMENT COLLECTION 74
TABLE 11 BUSINESS ANALYSIS TABLE 76
TABLE 12 SAMPLE RATIO CALCULATION TABLE.................... 82
TABLE 13 SAMPLE FINANCIALS ADJUSTMENT TABLE 83
TABLE 14 EXAMPLE OF RE-CONSTRUCTED FINANCIALS 86
TABLE 15 SAMPLE INCOME STATEMENT................................ 94
TABLE 16 SAMPLE BALANCE SHEET....................................... 95
TABLE 17 SAMPLE CASH FLOW STATEMENT 96
TABLE 18 SAMPLE OWNER FINANCING BUSINESS LOAN ANALYSIS... 114

TABLE 19 SAMPLE OWNER FINANCING BUSINESS LOAN
    ANALYSIS – LEASE TO OWN 119
TABLE 20 SAMPLE POOLING GROUP CONTRIBUTION & PAY-
    OUT TABLE 124

Preface

    Buying a business should not be only for experienced business owners or rich people. Given that the large corporations no longer guarantee employment, no one should rely on a job for retirement, education planning, savings or financial independence. With recent scandals throughout Corporate America, it is not even recommended to rely on a company's 401K plan as one's retirement savings vehicle. Over one trillion dollars in accumulated investors wealth and savings was lost when the Tech bubble collapsed.

    Investing in the stock market is a great way to save money for the future. But the stock market can only grow your invested capital by so much, and even that is not a guarantee that all your money will be preserved for future use. In addition, there is a possibility that the investor may loose all funds invested. However, if the markets rise, you may be able to increase the value of an investment, depending on what financial products were used as investment vehicles.

But what if you lost your job? Would the money invested in the market be enough to provide you with much needed cash flow to support yourself and your family? Unless you had accumulated a large sum of money, the answer will probably be No!

From our experience, one of the most efficient and rewarding ways to solve this problem is to own a business with good cash flow, and you can own that business while holding your day job. Do not believe that it is impossible to own a business while working for a big corporation. Actually, it is highly recommended, especially these days to follow such an approach. A lot of business owners do have good careers with large corporations. There was a story in the Wall Street Journal about a New Jersey bank CEO who owned several McDonald's franchises in addition to a real estate investment business, another one, the head of a large investment firm, is a partner in a chain of high-end restaurants. By owning a business, you are making sure that when / if you loose your job, you will have cash from the business to continue to support your needs. Having a business is the best way to generate cash that will actually grow to something that is significant enough to be invested in the Stock Market.

Although this tutorial was written as a guide for those who are thinking of owning a small business, existing owners who are thinking of expanding through the purchase of another business will benefit as well. It is a comprehensive handbook that will take the reader from the beginning of the process to the final stage of actually buying and owning an existing small business. It is written with the assumption that the buyer will have very little money for the acquisition, and so covers financing from a perspective that is totally different from that of similar books. Finally, although the material in this book will be very useful to an experienced owner or buyer, we are assuming that the reader is a first-time buyer who has never owned a business before.

Acknowledgements

This is the result of a lot of input, insight and guidance from many people. In particular, we want to thank our colleagues and many of our current and former clients and students who have shared their time, knowledge and experience over the past few years.

RGL Learning
New York City
June 2002

Introduction

Buying vs. Starting

First we need to warn the reader that buying a business does not provide one with the opportunity to spend more time with one's family and friends, does not necessarily allow for a better lifestyle, will be an all-consuming activity for several years after the purchase, and will use up all your time, and test your personal relationships.

The following ten paragraphs can help put things in perspective for the prospective buyer:

- In order to successfully run a business, you must have many skills and talents. You should be able to lead and make decisions quickly. You should work well with people and be totally committed to your mission regardless of the problems that you will encounter along the way. You should be able to absorb information quickly and work very long hours. Your family must support your venture and help along the road anyway possible.

- Experience in the industry into which you are buying should be a key driver behind the type of business you buy. Business owners care a great deal about the qualifications of someone who wants to buy their business. Not having experience (and money) in the field will give an owner second thought. Simply having enough cash to buy a business is not enough. The seller needs to know that you will be able to carry on. S/he will need to feel comfortable about the future of the employees who might have worked for the business for a long time. Establishing your credibility will increase the likelihood of your being considered a serious buyer.

- You should align yourself, if possible financially, with professionals (lawyers, brokers, accountants, etc.) who have experience in conducting business acquisition transactions. These individuals will guide you through the maze of compliance and regulatory issues that may come up along the way. If you can afford it, hire a good lawyer and a good account. An intermediary is a key ally, as s/he will ensure that you have access to quality businesses that are for sale, which you can afford.

- Money and credibility are necessary but not enough to buy a business. You also need to have a plan. A carefully thought out buyout or acquisition plan demonstrates that the buyer (or buying group) knows what is s/he wants to do and will make it easier to attract qualified help for the purchase.

- The majority of transactions for which a letter of intent has been signed, do not complete. So a serious buyer needs an aggressive search effort, which means that the acquirer has to be confident of his or her capabilities for the purchase. It also means pursuing several target businesses at the same time. Because a buyer has submitted a letter of intent to buy a business does not mean that s/he should stop searching. Until a transaction is closed, it is highly suggested that the buyer review several more potential acquisitions.

- Buying a business is a big undertaking that can require a considerable amount of capital, although in this book we cover ways to buy a business with little or no money. However, until the buyer knows what resources are at his or her disposal, s/he will not know which businesses are likely targets. If the buyer does not have any personal savings, we recommend spending a good deal of time searching for sources of funds. For example the buyer could dedicate time rallying friends and family, creating a Pooling Group (see Special Financing section later in the book), even forming a special investment club, in order to successfully close on the transaction. Having absolutely no money or sources of funds will result in a waste of everyone's time.

- Banks will generally require that new business owners personally guarantee loans. It is important for the prospective buyer to know his or her "Financial Elasticity" or strength. That is, to what extent can the buyer financially withstand the stress associated with a loan that has been called by the bank and therefore due to the lender immediately? To those who do not have the credit to qualify for such bank loans, do not be discouraged, however. This book was actually written with the assumption that the buyer may not be able to secure bank financing, and such details will be covered in the Financing section later on in this tutorial.

- Many people rely on a business owner: employees, customers, vendors, stockholders, bankers, etc. Your level of responsibility will go to the roof the minute you become a business owner. You will be facing payroll crisis, employee problems, customer satisfaction issues, a sizable debt load, etc. In addition, you will still be responsible for taking care of your family and meeting their needs. Furthermore, family members might have even invested in your new business. And that often creates situations of for extreme fiction. In other words, if your company starts to fail, or in fact fails, you as the owner will be the person ultimately in charge and responsible. Are you prepared to face such challenge?

- Buying a business is a long and tedious process. You have to deal with brokers, talk to suspicious business owners, take site visits, review business plans and analyze financials, in addition to raising money for the purchase and tending to your, and your family's, day-to-day life. And you might have to do all that for several businesses at the same time while keeping your day job. This requires patience, persistence and determination to achieve your goal. Many buyers become discouraged after a few months. The key is to be resilient and to keep on searching, even when you feel that you have seen all the businesses in town.

- Investing in a business is in some respect similar to investing in the stock market or real estate. Economic conditions might cause a buyer to pay too much for a business, and the interest rate on a loan (from bank or owner) may be too high. However, since no one can guarantee when an economic cycle will end, a buyer's best bet is to move forward with his or her plan for the purchase and not wait for better economic conditions. The key is to make sure that the business is a viable one that can navigate through both good and bad times, and that the business is worth the price you are willing to pay to acquire it.

In summary, buying a business is a daunting task. But the effort is well worth it as explained in the following three paragraphs:

- It is easier to find capital when acquiring a business. Buying a business that has been operating for 3 or more years, is profitable and has strong and good prospects, will definitely be easier to finance, especially if the buyer has experience in the industry.

- Statistics have proven that the failure rate for businesses that are acquired is far less than the failure rate of startup businesses, even when the purchaser does not have experience in the industry of the acquired business.

- Given that the business is already operating, the buyer can acquire the business as an absentee owner, keep the existing employees, and hold on to his/her current day job.

In essence, buying a business makes good economic sense for those who want to own a small business, be their own boss, or simply buy small businesses as an alternative investment strategy, instead of investing all their savings in the stock market.

Deciding on a Business to Purchase

Choosing an Industry

One of the most important elements in succeeding in business is to have experience in the field in which an entrepreneur wants to start or buy a business, unless an experienced manager will be hired to run the day-to-day operations of the business. What follows is a comprehensive list of industries that have been compiled to help the prospective buyer decide on an appropriate industry from which to buy his/her business. It is recommended to use a rating that is based on actual life or work experience, as well as knowledge of how a business operates in a particular industry. It is essential to be honest, as this will determine how successful you will be as a new business owner.

Rate yourself by placing a number from 0 to 9 next to the items listed below, with 9 being the best grade. On a separate piece of paper, take the time to elaborate on why you give yourself a grade of 6 or better for a particular segment. Information should include training received, job experience, affinity with natural habits, passion for the field, etc. At the end of this list select from 3 to 5 industries in which you think you would be successful. The industry (or industries) in which you should buy your business should match your skills and preferences as closely as possible. In the "Strong Points" column, use single words as opposed to sentences. If you find yourself easily finding key words that qualifies you for a particular sector, that may be a good sign to further investigate that industry, or simply drop it depending on your position with respect to that industry. Add any other industries that you feel are missing from this list.

If the reader has already decided on the industry from which to buy a business, this section can simply be skipped.

Table 1 Table of Industries

Industry

- Auto Dealerships
- Auto Stores and Distribution
- Autos and Auto-Related Auto/Truck Parts
- Broadcasting Radio Broadcasting
- Building and Construction Building Materials/Products
- Building/Construction Services
- Commercial Printing
- Consumer Finance
- Consumer Products/Food Alcoholic Beverages
- Convenience and Liquor Stores
- Cosmetics and Fragrances
- Dairy Products / Farms
- Department Stores
- Direct Marketing/Mail Order
- Do It Yourself Stores
- Drug Stores
- Dry Goods
- Educational Services
- Employment and Training Services
- Entertainment Film/TV Content
- Environmental Services
- Farm Products
- Finance/Specialty Finance Commercial Finance
- Financial Services
- Food Distribution
- Food Ingredients
- Food Miscellaneous

- Food Specialty Stores
- Footwear
- Forestry Related/Packaging Glass Packaging
- Frozen/Canned/Preserved Food
- Furniture and Fixtures
- General Entertainment
- Hardware: Desktop/Servers
- Hardware: Electronic Components
- Hardware: Enterprise
- Hardware: Peripherals
- Hardware: Storage Systems
- Home Furnishings/ Furniture Stores
- Home Health Care/Assisted Living
- Household Appliances
- Household Products
- Internet
- Lawn and Garden Equipment
- Lodging/Gaming Hotels/Motels/Casinos
- Magazine
- Media Stores
- Metal Packaging
- Movie Theaters
- Network & Systems Integration
- Newspapers
- Non-Alcoholic Beverages
- Non-Apparel Specialty Stores
- Nursing Home & Long Term Care
- Office and Photographic Equipment
- Office Products and Supplies
- Office Supply Stores
- Office/Store Furniture
- Outdoor Advertising
- Paging/Specialized Mobile Radio
- Paper Distribution
- Paper Packaging
- Paper Products

- Personal Care
- Personal Communications Services
- Pet Food
- Plastic Packaging
- Professional and Accounting Services
- Publishing Books
- Recorded Music
- Restaurants
- Retail Apparel
- Services Building and Cleaning Services
- Shipping
- Software Computer Software
- Supermarkets
- Technology Services: Professional Services
- Technology Services: Transaction Processing
- Tele-services
- Television Broadcasting
- Textile
- Tobacco
- Toys/Sporting Goods & Stores
- Trade Exhibitors
- Travel Services and Tourism
- Trucking & Transportation Services
- Vehicle Leasing / Rental
- Warehouse Clubs
- Wireless Cellular
- Wood Products

Researching an Industry

It is not necessary, and actually not recommended, to only choose one industry and use all resources to find a business in that particular industry. A better approach is to select, from the above list, a few sectors (between three and five) in which the potential buyer either has some experience or a strong desire to own a business.

However, experience and love of an industry are not a guarantee of success, if the buyer is lucky enough to find and acquire a business in that industry. Many aspects of an industry sector should be analyzed, regardless of personal experience or level of enthusiasm to own a business in a field. One important point to consider is whether an industry is in decay and will soon be replaced due to technological advances, or as may be requested by consumer demand.

So in making your choice, extreme care is required when analyzing a particular industry in which to buy a business. For the reader's convenience, we have included below a table to help facilitate the inquiry process. In addition, please keep in mind that certain industries, due to their nature, have better odds for success, even when the work itself may not be very enticing. For example, the US Chamber of Commerce has classified the following small business categories as the fastest growing small-business dominated industries:

- Restaurant

- Trucking, Transportation and Storage

- Outpatient Care Facilities and Physician Offices

- Supermarkets

- Special Trade Construction Contractors

- Computer and Data Processing Services, including Computer Schools and Training Centers

- Medical and Dental Laboratories

- Day Care Services

     As can be noted from the list above, these businesses are from sectors that fulfill consumers' and other businesses' everyday needs, and cannot be easily replaced by technological advances.

Goods have to be transported, consumers will always need to buy groceries, our children need to be taken care of when we go to work, etc. The potential buyer should view the acquisition of a business as a very long-term investment and plan the purchase accordingly.

Table 2 Industry Qualifying Table

Industry Name:

Notes:

Research Source:

Current Growth Rate:

Predicted Growth Rate (Past 5 yrs):

Projected Growth Rate (Next 5 yrs):

Finding a Business to Purchase

Acquisition Search

Finding the right business to buy will take time and patience. It usually takes from 6 months to 2 years to find the "perfect" acquisition opportunity. Some important points should be mentioned here before we go into the details of actually launching a methodical search.

First and foremost, do not stop your search simply because you have found a viable business to buy. In general, until the seller has signed your letter of intent (to be covered later), and you have started your due diligence process (also discussed later in the book), you should continue to look for more businesses to review and possibly purchase. Second, it is not necessary to stay focus on one industry. In fact, it is recommended that the serious buyer review many businesses in more than one industry (as was decided from the exercise in the previous section). This facilitates the search and opens up more options to the buyer. Third, make sure to screen out investigative sellers. These are business owners who do not need or want to sell, but are just feeling the market to find out how much they could get for their business if they decided to sell. Basically, they are using the serious buyer's interest to price their business.

That said, there are basically five ways to find businesses that are for sale: i) newspapers, ii) business brokers (also called intermediaries), iii) the Internet, iv) by calling or visiting owners of businesses in which the buyer has an interest, and v) direct marketing. The first three methods are what we will call the passive search, while in the last two, the prospective buyer takes a more proactive role in the search effort.

Newspaper

Finding businesses, especially small to mid-size businesses, in the classified sections of newspapers is very easy. The best place to look for businesses that are for sale is in the classifieds sections of newspapers that are distributed on Sundays. This also allows you to get a feel for what the market price is for comparable businesses in the area you are looking to buy. Good newspaper sources include the Sunday New York Times (see the 'Business Opportunities' section at the back of the 'Business' section), the Thursday edition of the Wall Street Journal, which also includes a special franchise section. In addition, the USA Today newspaper also has an extensive Business Opportunities section on Thursdays.

Note that a good source of business knowledge (market size, growth prospect, revenue potential, etc., for your industry can be found by researching, or even requesting a free information packet, from franchisers offering the type of business you want to purchase. You do not have to sign a Franchise Circular in order to receive such information. That means you are under no obligation when you receive such a package to buy the franchise. You simply want to use the information as a research reference.

Business Brokers

By looking under "Business Brokers" in your local Yellow Pages or on the Internet you will find many brokers in your neighborhood who are willing to help. Generally, it does not cost any money to "retain" their services and they have many contacts in their area of service that may facilitate your search for a business to purchase. It is recommended that you establish a relationship with at least three brokers in your immediate area. These brokers should be given very specific search criteria so that they can isolate those businesses that best meet you needs, preferences and financing capability.

Table 3 Sample Broker Specification Sheet

Business Type:
Business Category:

Gross Revenue ($)
Low End:

Ideal:

High End (if applicable):

Net Income
Low End:

Ideal:

High End (if applicable):

Asking Price
Low End:

Ideal:

High End (if applicable):

Location
Low End:

Ideal:

High End (if applicable):

Use this table (or a similar one) to give specific instructions to your brokers so that the search can be as efficient as possible. Your requirement might be in terms of business types (for example, Day Care Center, Laundromat, etc.) or business categories, such as Service, Manufacturing or Retail, although specifying business category (e.g. Service) may convey to your broker that you are not sure about what you are looking for.

Brokers tend to service buyers they believe are the most eager to buy a business. The way to convey your position to them is to follow-up on a regular basis for possible acquisition opportunities that you can review and/or visit. In addition, brokers usually feel a little uneasy about buyers who want to see just about every type of business. Although there is nothing wrong with looking at several types of businesses, it conveys the wrong message and a lack of focus. Brokers usually assume that the buyer is just "window-shopping" and is a waste of their time and effort. The best way to look at businesses from several sectors through business brokers is to work with several brokerage firms at the same time and ask each one to find you businesses that are from the different industries on which you have decided to focus.

Finally, be sure to contact your local real estate broker. These days, real estate agents have been acting as intermediaries for sellers of both properties and businesses. Such an approach makes sense for a Real Estate Brokerage firm because many businesses are being sold as part of a commercial building and most business brokers do not have the appropriate licensing and/or experience to sell real estate.

Please note that although brokers are a great source of businesses that are for sale in your search area, they tend to inflate prices in order to increase their commission. Prices presented by brokers to their buyers very often do not reflect the true value of a business. After all, brokers usually represent sellers and are not necessarily concerned about the buyer's position. So, careful analysis is required before submitting a 'Letter of Intent', or you might end up paying too much for a business (See "Valuation Analysis" later in the tutorial).

The Internet

These days, the best place to find small business acquisition opportunities is the Internet. The following web sites offer extensive lists of businesses that are for sale throughout the world. Some of them may require you to become a member of the site before you can view their listings for free. Some others may require you to pay.

Unless you have a sizable search budget, it is not recommended to pay for these services. You may be paying to view businesses that are no longer for sale, or simply not really for sale. If you are going to pay a web site to be able to view its listings of businesses that are for sale, you might as well pay to retain the services of a qualified business broker or M&A (Mergers and Acquisitions) specialist. In addition, note that most of these web sites ultimately refer you to a broker (or brokerage firm) who usually handles site visits, document request, meetings and negotiations with the owners.

Table 4 Web Sites Listing Businesses That Are For Sale

Web Site/
Brief Description

bizbuysell.com/
Launched on November 1, 1996, BizBuySell has grown to become the Internet's largest, most popular business-for-sale site with over 16,000 listings ranging from Ice Cream stores to dot com businesses

usbx.com/
USBX is building a new kind of Internet-enabled organization, dedicated to streamlining and expediting the M&A process. They provide a comprehensive set of M&A services through our core business units - M&A Advisory Services, Valuation Services, the Listing Exchange and the Resource Center.

empirebusinessbrokers.com/
With over 65+ offices worldwide, Empire Business Brokers is a network of hundreds of Business Brokers operating across the US, Canada, South America and Overseas. The firm is dedicated

to helping people to achieve the American Dream of owning their own small business with programs such as business brokering, franchise development and business financing.

gainsinc.com/
GAINS, Inc. is one of the largest Business Brokerage(s) in the world with headquarters in Manhattan's Times Square area and offices throughout the East Coast and Midwest. GAINS offers business opportunities in all major categories.

emerge.com/
Emerge Corporation was founded to provide marketplaces for the buyers and sellers of private businesses.

businessesforsale.com/
Provide a comprehensive range of services to facilitate the buying and selling of a business in the most effective manner possible.

ibba.org/
IBBA provides an extensive database of seller profiles to help a buyer find the right business.

cbex.com/
Provides online Mergers and Acquisitions services.

Nationlist.com/
Nation-List International is a network of nationwide brokers who help their clients in the purchase or sale of a business.

relocatable.com/
Re-locatable Business specializes in the sale of businesses that can be re-located at the buyer's wish.

Webmergers.com/
Webmergers.com is the leading provider of research and services for buyers and sellers of Internet and technology businesses.

Contacting Business Owners Directly

For prospective buyers who do not mind rejections and have a little bit more money to spend on an acquisition, approaching the owner of a business that is not for sale, is one of the best ways to buy a viable business. However, some owners might be offended by the unsolicited offer, or if s/he accepts to sell, might want much more for the business than it is actually worth.

But our experience has proven that most owners will sell a business when presented with the "right" price. If a buyer is willing to pay such a price, there might be some great acquisition opportunities waiting. Please note that when directly approaching the owner of a business that has not been put on the market for sale, one negotiation point (and maybe the only one) often used is the fact that there is no broker involved, and therefore no broker's commission.

It might be possible, if the buyer has managed to establish a good relationship with the seller, to reduce the asking price by the amount of money that the owner would have to pay to an intermediary. But again, it will not be easy. Often times, you convince an owner to sell a business that is working wonderfully and producing tremendous cash flow. If the owner is young, does not need immediate cash, and has a lot of family members working in the business, it may be close to impossible to consummate a transaction. However, it might be worth the effort put into approaching these business owners. Some brokers actually claim to do just that. They first find a buyer for a particular type of business and in a particular location, then they go out and try to convince an owner to sell.

One possible way for a prospective buyer to do that is to call a business owner first and, based on the result of a first conversation (if one actually took place), to schedule a face-to-face meeting. It is not recommended to simply show up at the door because business owners are extremely busy people who have no time for unscheduled and unsolicited visits. A little bit of research will help to find out the owner's name and the time s/he is usually in the office. In addition, it is highly recommended that the prospective buyer start using the services of the business that s/he has identified as a possible acquisition target, if not currently doing so. Once the buyer has collected basic information about the owner, and has used the services or products of the business, the first phone call may be placed. An initial conversation might start along the following lines:

"Hello Mr./Ms. [owner], I have been using your [services or products] for some time now and couldn't help calling to congratulate you. And actually, I was wondering if you would have a moment on [day] for me to stop by and introduce myself. I may have an interesting proposition for you concerning the future of your business..."

The caller's ability to raise the owner's curiosity and interest will determine what happens after that initial phone call.

Direct Marketing and Newspaper Advertising

The final two ways to reach business owners is to simply use direct mail marketing and small classified ads in the local newspapers.

<u>Classified advertising</u> is cheap and very effective. We would however, warn the reader that due to a possibly overwhelming amount of phone

calls, it is suggested that a separate phone number or voice-mail service be used. There is a lot more people who would love to sell their business than we realize. The best way to handle the responses to an ad is to allow for three to five days before returning phone calls. Some newspapers are so effective that they will generate calls two to three weeks after the ad's first appearance in the publication. In addition, some newspapers also publish their classified advertising section on their web site, giving more exposure to the advertiser. Once you believe that you have received most, or all calls from a particular ad, take a good hour or two to return all calls. Returning every single call is very important, as it is almost impossible to determine which one will result in a useful lead. In addition, about 50% of those phone calls will be from brokers. So you may want to call these last, or simply ignore them if you already have a good broker working for you. The following is a sample advertising copy of a small classified ad:

"Serious investor extremely interested in buying a small [Dry Cleaning] business in [your preferred] area. Ready to close right away. Call [your phone number]. Principals only [or, no brokers]."

Direct mail is a little bit more expensive than classified advertising in a buyer's efforts to find small businesses directly from owners. However, the efficiency of a direct mail campaign is certainly worth the added expense. Sending out a letter gives the potential buyer the opportunity to present him/herself with much more professionalism and will almost guarantee that the owner or potential seller will take the person more seriously. In addition, the direct mail letter allows the buyer to provide more details about the type of business that s/he is looking to buy, screening out much of the unwanted sellers. Furthermore, a mailing also guarantees that the buyer will not be receiving unnecessary calls from brokers. We recommend that the prospective buyer use a 9"x12" envelope as opposed to the regular size 10 envelopes which would require that the letter be folded. Using a larger envelope increases the odds that the mail will be open and read by the intended recipients. What follows is a sample letter that can be used to approach business owners:

Sample Copy For Direct Mail

Dear Business Owner:

This short letter is to express my strong interest in developing a strategic partnership, joint venture, or an outright purchase of your business. I am an independent investor and believe that your business might fit the profile of what I think would represent a good addition to my overall long-term investment portfolio.

What follows are two bulleted lists. The first one identifies the key characteristics of the ideal business with which I am looking to establish a relationship or buy. The second is a short summary of my background. I will call you within the next few days to confirm receipt of this letter and gauge you interest in possibly looking into this further.

Thanks for taking the time to read this letter and fell free to contact me if you have any questions.

Sincerely,

[You name]
[Your phone number]

Summary profile of a possible partner [Sample]

- Flatbed equipment
- Primary Routes: Northeast
- Commodities: building materials, steel
- Terminals: no more than 2 terminals located within the primary service area
- Equipment: 70% owner operator, 30% company owned
- Brokerage: up to 20% of total revenues brokered to other carriers

Resume summary [Sample for a Trucking Company]
- 50+ years of experience in the Transportation Industry
- Modern fleet of over 90 tractors and 150 trailers
- Safety standards that meets or exceeds ICC & DOT requirements
- Primary Service Are: Northeast (ME, NH, VT, MA, CT, NY)

End Sample Copy For Direct Mail

Tracking Leads

It is very important to keep good track of your acquisitions leads. You don't want to ask brokers for the same information twice. In addition, unless you keep all your newspapers, you will not be able to keep track of the business contacts you find in the "Business Opportunities" sections by simply circling the ads. Use the following form to manage what might grow into a sizable database of contacts. In addition, be sure to know what business sectors each one of your brokers will cover for you in order not to get confused when speaking to them. What follows is simply an example, please adapt it to reflect your specific needs for keeping track of information you gather.

Table 5 Sample Lead Tracking Sheet

Lead Tracking Sheet

Lead No.:
Date:
Lead Source:

General Business Information
Owner's Name:

Bus. Phone:

Business Address:

Due Diligence Details:

Valuation & Financials Details:

Offer & Negotiations Details:

Make copies of this form and use it to keep track of your progress

Determining the Condition of a Business

Due Diligence

Once you've isolated two or more businesses that most fit your search criteria, the next step is to draft a Letter of Intent and convey to the owners your intention to buy those businesses. Given that 50% of businesses that go into contract do not close, it is in your best interest to make more than one offer. This will guarantee that you end up with a business of your own after negotiations fail with the other sellers. Two samples of a 'Letter of Intent' have been included here for your convenience. The first one is a straight purchase letter. The second one is a variation of the first one that takes into account that there will be a leasing period before the assets are actually transferred to the new owner (See Financing section later on in this tutorial). Some sellers will allow a buyer to "try" the business before buying it. Leasing with an option to buy is analyzed in more details in the "Financing" section of this book.

Table 6 Sample Letter of Intent (I)

Sample Letter of Intent (I)
We, ([Buyer's Name] and whomever else I decide to take on as a partner for this purchase), propose to purchase all the assets of the [Business Name] located in [Business Location], including goodwill, customers, and all other intangible and balance sheet assets, to be substantially the same as those set forth on the balance sheet of the [Business Name] as of [Date Information was provided].

Sample Letter of Intent (I) *(Cont'd)*

1. Purchase Price: The purchase price for these assets will be payable in cash at closing as follows:
- $65,000 with all 28 machines in good working condition
- $62,500 with seven (7) machines to be repaired

We intend to pay for the business in the following way:
Pre-Closing:
- $650, Good faith deposit (We are assuming that the seller will accept the first option above)
At Closing:
- 20% of Asking price less $650 (Good Faith Deposit)
- 5% Seller note with repayment schedule to be determined (we will require that the seller carries a 5% note in order to close)
- 75% of Asking price from our Bank or other financing sources

2. Non-Competition Agreement: The owner of the Laundromat agrees not to compete, directly or indirectly, with this business for a period of one year after closing

3. Lease of Building Space: It is agreed that the owner will transfer the lease as specified in the

Sample Letter of Intent (I) *(Cont'd)*

business profile sheet we received (3 years + 5 year option)

4. General and Specific Liabilities: We will not assume any liabilities past, present, or future as they relate to the current and past operation of this Laundromat

5. Audit: We will ask a CPA to conduct an audit of the Laundromat's books at our expense

6. Expenses:

a) We and the owners of the Laundromat will each pay our own expenses, including legal expenses, up to the time of the closing.

b) In addition, we agree that no intermediary is involved in this transaction other than [Broker's Name], of [Broker's Company Name], whose compensation is the responsibility of the owner of the Laundromat

7. Letter of Intent: This letter of intent is non-binding and may not be construed as an agreement on the part of any party. In the event that the parties are unable to agree on a mutually satisfactory definitive agreement providing for the transactions contemplated by this letter of intent, none of the parties shall be liable to any other party or to any other person. The

Sample Letter of Intent (I) *(Cont'd)*

conclusion of any definitive agreement will be subject to the following:

a) Approval of all matters relating thereto by the Laundromat's owner's and our lawyers

b) Review of all business, legal, and auditing matters related to the Laundromat, the results of which are acceptable to us

c) Completion of such financing as we may require to effect a closing; Preparation and completion of all closing documents.

d) The closing date to take place in or within 60 days of the execution of this agreement.

8. Continuing Obligations: Until termination of this letter of intent, the seller should not entertain negotiations with or make disclosures to any other party, without prior consent of buyer.

9. Confidentiality: Both the buyer and the seller agree to maintain complete confidentiality regarding this transaction.

All documents in respect to this transaction will be prepared by our attorney, subject to such

Sample Letter of Intent (I) *(Cont'd)*

documents being reviewed by and being acceptable to the seller's legal counsel

Buyer
    Print Name:
    Signature:

Seller
    Print Name:
    Signature:

Broker
    Print Name:
    Signature:

Date:

End Sample Letter of Intent (I)

Table 7 Sample Letter of Intent (II)

===
Sample Letter of Intent (II)
(This sample assumes a Lease to Buy option & includes a Memorandum of Understanding as well as the Letter of Intent)
===

Memorandum of Understanding
Dated December 18, 2001

This binding Memorandum of Understanding is by and between [Buyer's Name] located at [Buyer's Address] (hereinafter referred to as Buyer) and [Seller's Name] (hereinafter referred to as Seller) owner of Laundromat located at [Address of Business]. No Broker or Intermediary is representing Seller.

Buyer proposes to acquire from Seller, all the assets of the Laundromat located at [Address of Business] through a two-step process, as follows:
- A Leasing & Extended Due Diligence Phase (see below for details)
- The Purchase and Transfer of the Laundromat Assets for the Full Asking Price of $50,000 (see Letter of Intent attached)

Leasing and Extended Due Diligence Phase
Buyer will purchase Laundromat from Seller for the full Asking Price ($50,000), as proposed in the attached Letter of Intent, if Seller agrees to lease the business to Buyer for a period of three (3) months AND receive the down payment ($25,000) after this extended due diligence period.

Down payment amount of $25,000 will be paid to Seller in cash or cashier's check.

Payments for the $25,000 balance will be in the form of a
===

Sample Letter of Intent (II) *(Cont'd)*

Note due to Seller starting one month after the beginning of the Leasing & Extended Due Diligence Phase at the rate of $471.78 per month. (See Letter of Intent below for details) The Terms of this Leasing and Extended Due Diligence Phase will be as follows:
- Seller agrees to hold and keep possession of the facility's Leasing Agreement with the landlord, until after 3 months when the $25,000 down payment is received and business assets transferred to Buyer
- Buyer agrees to keep the Laundromat running as is (or better, when/if improvements are possible)
- Buyer also agrees to retain all employees and keep same store operating hours
- If Seller agrees with the above sale structure and the Letter of Intent below, Buyer is ready to move forward immediately (within the next 5 days). The following will be needed to proceed:
- Past two years financials from Seller, including utilities bills (2-3 days)
- Employee payroll information (1 day)
- Execution of the Letter of Intent with the assistance of each party's attorney (1 day)
- A one day training session by Seller marking the begin of the Leasing & Extended Due Diligence Phase (3 months)

Letter of Intent To Purchase Business

We, ([Buyer's Name] and whomever else I decide to take on as a partner for this purchase), propose to purchase all the assets of the Laundromat located at [Address of

Sample Letter of Intent (II) *(Cont'd)*

Business], including goodwill, customers, and all other intangible and balance sheet assets, to be substantially the same as those set forth on the balance sheet of the Laundromat as of submission date before the start of the Leasing and Extended Due Diligence Phase.

1. Purchase Price: The purchase price for these assets will be the full asking price of $50,000 to be paid as follows:
Down Payment (Due after 3 months of Leasing & Extended Due Diligence Phase):
- 50% of full Asking price: $25,000 in cash or cashier's check
Seller Note:
- 50% ($25,000) Seller note with repayment scheduled over five (5) years at a rate of 5%, for 60 monthly payments of $471.78. Payments will start one month after beginning of Leasing & Extended Due Diligence Phase, although down payment will not be due until after that extended period
Important Note: If after the Leasing Period, data collected by Buyer have a severe negative variation (more than 10%) from financial data provided by Seller, Buyer reserves the right to re-negotiate the purchase price OR cancel this Letter of Intent. In the even that the Letter of Intent is cancelled, Buyer agrees to pay back to Seller all profits (if any) realized during the 3-month Leasing period. Such amount will be due within one day of cancellation of the Letter of Intent.
2. Non-Competition Agreement: Seller agrees not to compete, directly or indirectly, with this business for a

Sample Letter of Intent (II) *(Cont'd)*

period of one year after closing

3. Lease of Building Space: It is agreed that Seller will transfer the lease as specified in the business profile sheet received by Buyer

4. General and Specific Liabilities: Buyer will not assume any liabilities past, present, or future as they relate to the current and past operation of this business

5. Audit: Buyer will ask a CPA to conduct an audit of the business' books at his expense

6. Expenses:

a) Buyer and Seller will each pay their own expenses, including legal expenses, up to the time of the closing (After 3-month Leasing period).

b) In addition, Seller agrees that compensation for any intermediary or broker involved in this transaction is sole the responsibility of Seller

7. Letter of Intent: This letter of intent is non-binding and may not be construed as an agreement on the part of any party. In the event that the parties are unable to agree on a mutually satisfactory definitive agreement providing for the transactions contemplated by this letter of intent, none of the parties shall be liable to any other party or to any other person. The conclusion of any definitive agreement will be subject to the following:

a) Acceptance by Seller of Buyer's Leasing & Extended Due Diligence Phase.

b) Approval of all matters relating thereto by the Seller's and Buyer's lawyers

c) Review of all business, legal, and auditing matters related to the business, the results of which are acceptable

Sample Letter of Intent (II) *(Cont'd)*

to Buyer
d) Completion of such financing as may be required to effect a closing; Preparation and completion of all closing documents.
e) The closing date to take place in or within 90 days of the execution of this agreement, immediately (within 1 day) after the Leasing & Extended Due Diligence Phase.
8. Continuing Obligations: Until termination of this letter of intent, the Seller should not entertain negotiations with or make disclosures to any other party, without prior consent of Buyer. In other words, this business should be taken off the market.

9. Confidentiality: Both the Buyer and the Seller agree to maintain complete confidentiality regarding this transaction.
10. Buyer Training: Seller agrees to assist Buyer for a period of 45 days (one month and 15 days) on an as-needed basis. That includes the above-mentioned one-day on-site training session.
All documents in respect to this transaction will be prepared by Buyer's attorney, subject to such documents being reviewed by and being acceptable to the Seller's legal counsel

---
Sample Letter of Intent (II) *(Cont'd)*

Buyer
    Print Name:
    Signature:

Seller
    Print Name:
    Signature:

Broker
    Print Name:
    Signature:

Date:

End of Sample Letter of Intent (II)

However, signing a letter of intent to purchase a business does not mean that the buyer is locked into acquiring the business. The letter is simply one step that alerts the seller that the buyer is serious about acquiring the business and will do that if Due Diligence proves the business worthwhile.

Such a letter should also include clauses that will make it possible for the buyer to get out of the transaction if necessary. Among causes most frequently used for that purpose are: failure to secure financing, inability to come to a final consensus on the price, discrepancies between data provided by the seller and results obtained through actual review of the operations, legal problems, assumption of the business debt, etc.

This is why Due Diligence, the subject of this section, is such an important step when buying a business. It is absolutely imperative that the prospective buyer (or buying group, in the case of an Investment Club or Pooling Group) runs a thorough check to determine the condition of a business that s/he intends to acquire. Sellers may want to sell because the business is inherently flawed and is on the verge of collapsing. Even when the business is in good standing, the owner may be trying to hide something from the prospective buyer. Just like real estate, when buying a business the investor needs to run a series of checks and balances to ensure that the business is indeed in good standing and operating properly.

What follows is a list of important items that must be thoroughly investigated. Each item is accompanied by a brief synopsis of what has to be verified. Our advice to any entrepreneur contemplating buying a business is that all of the items listed below should be investigated to ensure that the business being acquired is a good operating enterprise. You do not want to be investing your hard-earned money into a failing business.

Do not casually run through the list below. If necessary, or if you have the funds, hire a professional with business investigation expertise. Your due diligence will ensure that you uncover anything that is being hidden from you by the seller. And that's why it is extremely important to make sure that there are clauses in your letter of intent that make your purchase contingent upon satisfactory due diligence results, That is, results with which you, your lawyer and/or account are satisfied.

Note that not all of these items will apply for all businesses. The reader should use the ones that make the most sense for the target business and industry.

==
Table 8 Due Diligence Table I

Due Diligence Item: Financials
Item to investigate:
a) Balance Sheet, Income & Cash Flow Statements. These will be analyzed in depth in the special 'Valuation Analysis' section, later in this book. They are the most important documents of your Due Diligence package as they will tell

you whether or not the business is growing, stagnant or failing. Usually 3 to 5 years are required in order to make a good analysis of the business. Never buy a business that is loosing money, unless you have the financial muscles and resources, as well as the expertise to turn it around.
b) Undisclosed debts and liens against business assets by running a UCC (Uniform Commercial Code) search

Target Date:
Done (Y/N):
===

Due Diligence Item: General Company History
Item to investigate:
a) Overview of founding and evolution of the Company
b) Significant events since the date of founding (e.g. previous acquisitions or subsidiary/location sale)
c) Rationale for selling Company (why is the owner selling?)
d) Special aspects of the business (is it a regional or cyclical business?)

Target Date:
Done (Y/N):
===

Due Diligence Item: Business Structure/General Legal Documents **Item to investigate:**
a) Basic legal structure (Sole proprietorship,
Corporation, etc.). That will affect whether the transaction is executed as a stock or assets sale. See "Legal Issues" section
b) Organization charts (if applicable)
c) Certificates of incorporation

Target Date:
Done (Y/N):
===

Due Diligence Item: Industry
Item to investigate:
a) Growth Trends (you do not want to buy a
business in a dying industry)
b) Cyclicality of business or products (overall economy, seasonal)
c) Future outlook
d) Market analysis (size, trends, etc.)
e) Barriers to entry (how easy is it for a competitor to get into this business?)
f) Review available market research or industry analysis

Target Date:

Done (Y/N):

Due Diligence Item: Competition
Item to investigate:
a) Main competitors (by product segments, geographic, regions, etc.)
b) Prospective competitors
c) Sales approach (how do your prospective competitors market their products or services compared to your seller?)
d) Product positioning (price, technology)

Target Date:
Done (Y/N):

Due Diligence Item: Competitive Advantages
Item to investigate:
a) Source of uniqueness
b) Market share
c) Brand name
d) Economies of scale
e) Changing technologies

Target Date:
Done (Y/N):

Due Diligence Item: Products
Item to investigate:
a) Review existing products or services
b) List major customers for each product
c) List of major competitors for each product/service
d) Profile potential new entrants and their new products/services
e) Analyze nature of competition (efficacy, price)

Target Date:
Done (Y/N):

Due Diligence Item: Suppliers
Item to investigate:
a) What method is used to purchase principal items
b) How far ahead does the company purchase inventories
c) Who are the major suppliers (top 10)?
d) What is your source of materials, including contracts, any minimum purchase contracts, purchase orders for significant items of purchase and sole source suppliers?

e) Are there any special discounts?

Target Date:
Done (Y/N):

==

Due Diligence Item: Sales organization
Item to investigate:
a) Structure
b) Size
c) Compensation (salaried vs. commission, incentives, etc.)
d) Training

Target Date:
Done (Y/N):

== **Due Diligence Item:** Marketing strategy
Item to investigate:
a) Types of advertising/promotional activity
b) Pricing
c) Trends of expenditures
d) How does this strategy differ (or not) from competitors?

Target Date:
Done (Y/N):

== **Due Diligence Item:** Distribution
Item to investigate:
a) Distribution mechanics
b) Areas served
c) Significant agreements/arrangements
d) Outlets: **i)** Types and % of volume distributed through each (by county or region if applicable); **ii)** Facilities (location and % of volume shipped from each); **iii)** How does this distribution differ (or not) from competitors?

Target Date:
Done (Y/N):

==

End Table 8 Due Diligence Table I

==

This might look somewhat overwhelming to someone buying a business for the first time. But the prospective buyer should not proceed until satisfactory Due Diligence has been completed. And that process can take from 1 week to 3 months or more, depending on the size and complexity of the business being acquired. Even though we do not want to paralyze ourselves with analysis, reviewing the most relevant items on this list for your particular industry is highly recommended and will virtually guarantee that the business you buy is worth your invested capital.

For example, if you were going to purchase a wholesale business, you would need to make sure that the following Due Diligence Items are totally investigated before finalizing your offer:

Table 9 Due Diligence Table II

Item To Investigate/ Notes

Financials
See Valuation Analysis in the following section.

Industry
You do not want to buy a business where technological advance or a better product is

replacing the product that the target business distributes, unless you can plan to distribute or sell that new product. As discussed previously, the industry you are buying into is critical, as its prospects will determine whether you are making a long- or short-term investment. You need to be in a sector where your services will be needed for a least the next five to seven years without major industry shakeout. Although it is difficult to predict, basic research can provide the data necessary to figure out if there are any major changes under way in a particular industry. If that is the case, unless you believe that you will have the required funds to weather out the storm and make necessary changes to your operations, it is recommended that the buyer get into a business that will be more stable within the next few years,

Competition

You never want to buy a business without a thorough analysis of your current and possible future competitors' strategy. Among the most important points you will need to be aware of are your competitors' pricing levels, advertising medium, marketing channels, vendors and special promotions. You want to be able to match what they do with either a variation of what they offer, or a new and improved product or service.

Suppliers
You want to make sure that you will continue to get the products you sell from the suppliers. The worst thing that can happen to a buyer is to find out after an acquisition that the acquired business' major supplier will no longer sell its products to the business after the new buyer take over. No one should buy a business if they can not establish a solid relationship with their future suppliers. They are part of the lifeblood of the business as they provide the owner with what the customers need.

Sales
The prospective buyer must confirm sales data from a seller. That can be accomplished in many ways, but can usually be verified by inspecting purchase orders and receipts from suppliers. The more products are purchased from suppliers, and the more often they are purchased, the more they are being sold. A business that has a high level of sales is always ordering new merchandise to re-stock its inventory reserves. This will be your clue as to whether sales have been stagnant, increasing, or decreasing. Of course if there is a lot of buying activities in the immediate months preceding the sale of the business, there could be ground for further investigation as the owner might have been "preparing" the business' financials for the sale.

The other important clue that can help a buyer gauge sales level is the activities in the business' bank account. The prospective buyer should inspect frequency and size of deposits for several weeks prior to the Due Diligence period. Please note that it is even more important to inspect bank statements of service businesses where no inventory has to be purchased. (Dry Cleaning businesses are a good example of a service business that does not have to buy any inventory for re-sale.)

Distribution
Distribution is one of the most important factors that can make or break a small business, especially a small business in the wholesale industry. Items to inspect will vary from increasing distribution cost (a red flag) to actual distribution channel, like postal mail, the Internet, independent distributors, etc.

End of Table 9 Due Diligence Table II

If a buyer is reluctant to conduct a thorough Due Diligence, there are software packages that can help to analyze an acquisition (see the Appendix for additional resources for prospective business buyers). Or, you can simply hire the services of an expert if you have the funds to do so.

However, most prospective small business buyers do not have the financial resources to do that. So, simply studying the material covered in this section and following the advice and steps outlined in this book will almost guarantee that you will not be buying a failing business.

Determining The Price To Pay For A Business

Valuation Analysis

For simplicity's sake, this book will assume that the buyer will be acquiring a single business with possibly more than one location (for example a small Laundromat business with two locations). In addition, we will not be covering valuation techniques for businesses where more than one product line or service will be acquired. For the purpose of this discussion, we will assume the simplest of all cases. For example if a buyer is acquiring a retail business, that business will be assumed to sell one type of product (for example, children's clothing). This book is also assuming that its reader will be buying, or intends to buy, a small business that is privately held and valued at $1MM or less.

Finally, we will be focusing on valuing a business that is not going to be turned around, but will continue to operate (or grow) as purchased, under the new owner. A business that is failing and in need of an experienced buyer to re-structure and turn it around, or fix it, has to be valued using a different set of valuation metrics. Note that even though there are many ways to value a business, to keep things simple, and in light of its audience, this book will be using a straight forward multiple of earnings (net income) method to help a buyer arrive at a value that is as close as possible to the intrinsic value of the business. But keep in mind that in the end a business' value is equal to what a buyer is willing to pay and a seller willing to accept.

To analyze a business, we begin by collecting and reorganizing its accounting and financial statements. Below is a list of essential documents that need to be gathered and analyzed. To make this analysis worthwhile, financials statements for at least the past three years must be available, preferably on a monthly basis. We recommend buying a business that has been operating (and has been profitable) for at least three full years:

Table 10 Valuation Document Collection

Document Description
Income statement (Profit and Loss)
Balance sheet (Assets and Liabilities)
Cash flow statement
Monthly bank statements
Equipment list with replacement value
List of customers and contracts (with length of time left on contracts)
Employee roster with description of responsibility and salary information
Owners' percentage interest along with salary and benefits information (health, insurance, company car, etc.)

Copy of lease agreement

Lines of credit, if applicable

End of Valuation Document Collection

Note that most brokers and owners will require that you sign a confidentiality agreement and put down a "good-faith" (different from a down payment) deposit before you are given access to such confidential information. That is normal procedure and you should be ready to remit at least 0.50% of your offer price (not the owner's asking price) to the broker to be put in escrow. Some brokers use a fixed amount (e.g. $1,000). That amount is used as proof that you are serious about buying the business and will either be:
- Deducted from the final sale price if you buy the business, or
- Refunded to you in full by the broker, if you decide to not proceed with the acquisition

Before going into the actual analysis phase, it is worth mentioning that before jumping into complicated evaluation, it is extremely important to think about the context of a purchase. The overall timing of a potential business purchase has to be thought through. Even if the business is a great one, a purchase at the peak of an economic down cycle may not be the right thing to do. A good business in a bad industry is definitely not recommended. Finally an analysis of the market in which a business participates needs to be performed to uncover what really drives the business. The following is a list of issues that have to be considered while the valuation analysis is being performed:

Table 11 Business Analysis Table

Issue to Consider/ Resulting Notes
Business environment & government regulations
Business cycle impact
Geographical risk
Cost structure (including material and labor)
Ease of financing (for internal growth or acquisition)

State of facilities and equipment

Competitors & potential entrants

Channels of distribution

Customer needs and their Characteristics

Flexibility in pricing your product or service (e.g. can you increase the number of coins needed to use a washing machine in a Laundromat without changing the machine itself?)

Your strength as the new owner, including your age and experience

Technology needs

Advertising and promotion needs

===
Legal issues and potential liabilities

===
Expansion opportunities (or lack thereof)

===
End of Business Analysis Table
===

Working With The Financial Statements

A few words of caution: Some brokers will provide you with both original financials as well as their version of a set of re-cast financials for the business they are trying to sell. Do not rely on these numbers to make your offer. Brokers generally try to inflate the asking price in order to increase their fee. Unless you can hire your own valuation specialist, follow the instructions in this section to do your own analysis of the business.

Owners of privately held businesses are very motivated to pay the least amount of taxes possible. To achieve that goal, and to the extent permitted by accounting standards, they manipulate their expense accounts in order to show on paper that the business is making the least amount of profit possible. That, in turn, lowers their tax liability on the business' net income. To objectively value a business, its financials have to be reconstructed, or re-calculated. That is, adjustments have to be made to reflect the true profit potential of that business. Such adjustments are sometimes called add backs.

Examples of such abnormal expense items by business owners include extremely large bonuses or salaries to themselves, above-market rent space from a building that is family-owned, and company cars that are used for personal use. Sometimes such expenses may include illegitimate items such as salaries for non-working family members, family vacations marked as business trips, and personal expenses charged to the company. This leads us to conclude that some of these expenses have to be adjusted or re-calculated in context. The prospective buyer can do that by using either (or both) of the following:

- Good business judgment based on experience in the industry, or
- Standard expense multiples (or ratios) for the industry in question

The simplest and cheapest way to get such industry data is to review comparable data from publicly held companies that are in the same industry or line of business. Such information is freely available on the Internet and can be downloaded from web sites such as Yahoo!Finance, sec.gov, or any financial web site for which there is no fee for reviewing such information. In addition, all publicly traded companies have their financials posted on their own web site under "Investor Relations". For example, if you're planning to buy a retail clothing business, you may want to look at the income statements of companies such as Gap, Inc., Abercrombie & Fitch Co., Children's Place Retail S, Chico's FAS, Inc.,etc., and taking an average of their individual ratios.

Unless the buyer can purchase data for such an analysis, information obtained from the financials statements of publicly held companies are the most accurate way to measure industry ratios (even the IRS agrees with this valuation method through its Revenue Ruling 59-60). The rationale behind it is that public companies have to try extremely hard to keep expenses in line. That is because they have a duty to report to their shareholders, in addition to helping raise their stock price by encouraging investors to buy shares of the company. That effectively results in more realistic numbers when it comes to business expenses.

Multiples are usually calculated by dividing the actual line item expense, either by the company's total revenue, or net income, as long as you keep the divider the same throughout the exercise. For example, to create a ratio for Travel & Entertainment (T&E) the buyer can divide the total amount spent on T&E by the total company revenue. This ratio can then be applied to your own analysis by multiplying it to the T&E expense of your acquisition target. The difference from the number supplied by the Owner and the result from applying the ratio would be used as a T&E add back to be added to the net income. The above step has to be done for each add back item. In the illustration table included in this section, the buyer's analyst used the following add back items for the analysis:

- Salary / Compensation
- Repairs / Maintenance
- Office Expenses
- T&E
- Automobile
- Personal Insurance
- Family Relations

- Misc. Expenses

Table 12 Sample Ratio Calculation Table

Ratio Computation Table For 3 Companies & 1 Expense Line (e.g. Office Expenses)

Company 1

Expense 1:

Revenue 1 (or Net Income):

Ratio 1 = (Expense 1 / Revenue 1):

Company 2

Expense 2:

Revenue 2 (or Net Income):

Ratio 2 = (Expense 2 / Revenue 2):

Company 3

Expense 3:

Revenue 3 (or Net Income):

Ratio 3 = (Expense 3 / Revenue 3):

Average Ratio: (R1+R2+R3) / 3

Once ratios have been calculated using the sample table above, it is time to start reconstructing the company's financials by applying the derived ratios to original amounts found in the Financial Statements received from the owner (see sample statements below). The amounts obtained by applying the ratios are subtracted from the original expense line values to deduct the adjusted amounts. Use the table below or a similar one to facilitate this exercise. Note that it is recommended to do the above exercise using at least 5 companies from the industry into which the buyer is looking to purchase.

Table 13 Sample Financials Adjustment Table

In this table, ratios can be calculated by dividing total revenue by each one of the line items below. Note that Revenue in this context refers to the revenue of a public company that is being used in the benchmark. Data for this exercise can be obtained by visiting the Internet (e.g., Yahoo!Finance). It is recommended that the buyer calculate at least 5 ratios and use the average to extract a more representative ratio.

Salary
    Original:
    Ratio:
    Adjusted:
    Addback (Original – Adjusted):

Repairs
>*Original:*
>*Ratio:*
>*Adjusted:*
>*Addback (Original – Adjusted):*

Office Exp.
>*Original:*
>*Ratio:*
>*Adjusted:*
>*Addback (Original – Adjusted):*

T & E
>*Original:*
>*Ratio:*
>*Adjusted:*
>*Addback (Original – Adjusted):*

Automobile
>*Original:*
>*Ratio:*
>*Adjusted:*
>*Addback (Original – Adjusted):*

Insurance
>*Original:*
>*Ratio:*
>*Adjusted:*
>*Addback (Original – Adjusted):*

Family
> *Original:*
> *Ratio:*
> *Adjusted:*
> *Addback (Original – Adjusted):*

Misc. Exp.
> *Original:*
> *Ratio:*
> *Adjusted:*
> *Addback (Original – Adjusted):*

Total (add to original net income):

Once reasonable multiples have been applied, the differences should be added back to the income statement of the business. This will result in a noticeable increase in net profit, or a decrease in net loss, from the Income Statement. As can be seen in the case below, there is a sizable gap between the Net Income on the left and the Adjusted Earnings on the right. That adjusted number reflects a more likely income from the business' operations if the owner did not have to minimize income in order to reduce payment of business taxes. To help understand this better, the reader should thoroughly familiarize him/herself with the example provided below. It was taken from the Valuation Analysis of a small chain of technology training schools, which the author was advising.

Table 14 Example of Re-Constructed Financials

Re-Constructed Financials - New York

New York (000) – '00
Tuition Revenues: $4,026
Other Income/(Refund): $0
Cost of Sales: $(139)
Operating Expenses: $(3,615)
Other Expenses: $(120)
Net Income: $151

Addback(000) - '00
Salary: $250
Repairs: $11
Office Exp.: $75
T&E: $50
Automobile: $15
Insurance: $15
Family: $25
Misc.: $70
  Adjusted Earnings: $513

  Once you have constructed an adjusted earning from the business' financials, pricing can be made quite simple. We recommend that the buyer apply a multiple ranging from 1.5x to 3.5x, to the Adjusted Earnings. Using such multiples, a buyer is essentially paying a seller for the right to collect the business operating earnings in the future. Assuming that the business continues to operate forever, the buyer is basically buying an unlimited amount of future cash for 1.5x to 3.5x its current net income. For example if your adjusted earnings are $50,000, your offer price might be between $75,000 and $175,000, depending on how strongly you feel about owning the business and the amount of cash you have to spend. However, if the business operates for the next ten years, for example, and continues to produce the same (or more) amount of cash, the buyer's potential total income from the transaction could be $500,000 ($50,000*10) or more.

Note that it is important to pay close attention to the prices of comparable businesses in the area where your target business is located. Also, note that the multiples suggested above are simply guidelines. You may want to pay more or less, depending on how strongly you feel about the business' prospects and future growth, and how you've structured the transaction with the seller.

The reader might be asking why such emphasis on the Net Income of a business as opposed to just valuing its assets. The truth is that, in addition to the fact that some businesses, such as certain service businesses, do not have any hard assets, assets do not produce cash flow, revenue and income do. Although the assets of a business are important, if they are not generating enough cash flow, they can not help the buyer cover business expenses.

In addition, a business can generally find ways to generate revenues that its assets are not capable of producing. For example, a computer manufacturer may, in addition to selling computers, decide to provide computer maintenance services to its clients. Another example might be a Laundromat owner who decides to provide Dry Cleaning services by contracting out the work to a Dry Cleaning Plant. In both cases, the assets of the businesses (e.g. computers, washers and dryers) do not produce the income received. Because the buyer is acquiring the right to receive the future earnings of the business, its ability to produce cash is really what is important.

As we can see, having your offer price dependent upon the true income (or income potential) of the business is essential. If your value is too low and you are unable to negotiate with the seller, you may be missing on a great opportunity. On the other hand, if your analysis results in overpricing the business, you will be paying too much for a business that may fail after you have invested possibly all of your life savings into it.

Additional Valuation Tips

Using the multiple of earnings discussed above presents a very simple way to extract the value of any business after its financials have been analyzed and re-constructed. However, sometimes, it may be necessary to adjust that technique into a more specialized form of valuation, as briefly discussed below, depending on the type of business that is being purchased. To address that issue, the following sections will briefly introduce some of the details that may be involved in valuing certain types of businesses or assets. A buyer involved in any one of those businesses may first want to apply the multiple of earnings method and then apply necessary adjustments.

Valuing Intangible Assets

When buying a business it is very important to recognize that there may be several factors and things that contribute to the business income and profit. Among the most common items that must be taking into the analysis are:

- Software system
- Patents
- Trademark
- Copyrights
- Subscriptions
- Customers
- Contracts (both government and corporate)
- Brand names

The above items make up a company's Intangible Assets and must be factored into the valuation analysis because they often play an important role in revenue generation. Although there are no rules-of-thumb when valuing intangible assets, it may be pointed to the reader that these assets are usually analyzed using one of the following methods:

- Determining what it would cost another business to duplicate a given asset today
- Measuring the benefits intangible assets will bring to a business, and how long those benefits will last
- Predicting the life span and future financial benefits of an intangible asset

Professional Practice Valuation

Professional practices such as accounting, consulting, law and medical practice firms, are usually assets light. But strong relationships with their customers and highly trained employees are extremely valuable. A firm's customers must be reviewed closely to determine how much value can be attributed to those customers. Usually the length of the relationships will be a key point as stability and longevity are two signs of lower risk, and hence higher value.

Final Note about Valuation and Premiums Payments

Even though this book is targeted at buyers of privately held businesses (a premium is almost always required with the acquisition of a publicly held company), we would like to mention that many times, there might be a need to add a premium to the resulting asking price from a valuation analysis. That is, a buyer may have to pay the seller an amount above the fair value of the business to make up for certain factors such as:

- Contracts (especially government contracts),

- Goodwill (an intrinsic value attached to the business as a running entity),

- Hard assets (except for real estate which is normally valued separately from the business),

- Patents, and

- Exclusivity (applicable normally to transportation or distribution businesses)

In such cases, the premium to be paid will be based on industry standard, the buyer's judgment, and his/her level of interest in the business.

In addition, if the business is a really great business and the Intermediary or broker had done a good job at promoting it for the buyer, there may be more than one buyer interested in buying that business. In that case, an auction may result with the best price and most qualified buyer closing on a transaction with the seller.

Table 15 Sample Income Statement

Period Ending: Mar 31, 2002
Total Revenue: $6,113,986
Cost Of Revenue: $1,796,435
Gross Profit: $4,317,551

Operating Expenses
Research/Development: $0
Selling/Admin. Expenses: $3,830,256
Non Recurring: $0

Operating Income: $487,295
Total Net Expenses: $4,323
Earnings Before Interest And Taxes: $491,618
Interest Expense: $50,473
Income Before Tax: $441,145
   Income Tax Expense: $118,000
   Equity Earnings Or Loss Unconsolidated
Subsidiary: $0
   Minority Interest: $0
Net Income: $323,145

Non-recurring Events
   Discontinued Operations: $0
   Extraordinary Items: $0
   Effect Of Accounting Changes: $0
Net Income: $323,145
   Pref. Stock & Other Adj.: ($296,628)

Table 16 Sample Balance Sheet

Period Ending - Mar 31, 2002

Current Assets
Cash And Cash Equivalents: $1,824,808
Short Term Investments: $0
Net Receivables: $3,275,895
Inventory: $261,000
Other Current Assets: $304,485
Total Current Assets: $5,666,188

Long Term Assets
Long Term Investments: $100,000
Property Plant & Equipment: $1,532,738
Goodwill: $6,469,113
Intangible Assets: $39,182
Accumulated Amortization: $0
Other Assets: $289,978
Deferred Long Term Asset Charges: $0
Total Assets: $14,097,199

Current Liabilities
Accounts Payable: $3,476,993
Short & Long Term Debt: $199,969
Other Current Liabilities: $4,220,900
Total Current Liabilities: $7,897,862
Long Term Debt: $979,311
Other Liabilities: $858,253

Deferred Long Term Liability: $43,549
Minority Interest: $0
Negative Goodwill: $0

Total Liabilities: $9,778,975

Stock Holders Equity
Misc. Stocks Options Warrants: $0
Redeemable Preferred Stock: $0
Preferred Stock: $13,264,236
Common Stock: $450
Retained Earnings: ($31,223,773)
Treasury Stock: ($148,469)
Capital Surplus: $22,425,780
Other Stockholder Equity: $0
Total Stockholder Equity: $4,318,224

Net Tangible Assets: ($2,150,889)

Table 17 Sample Cash Flow Statement

Period Ending: Mar 31, 2002
Net Income: $323,145

Cash Flow Operating Activities
Depreciation: $190,063
Adjustments To Net Income: ($14,883)

Changes in Operating Activities
Changes In Accounts Receivables: ($1,391,169)
Changes In Liabilities: $247,684

Changes In Inventories: $0
Changes In Other Operating Activities: ($25,086)
Cash Flows From Operating Activities: ($670,246)

Cash Flow Investing Activities
Capital Expenditures: ($84,025)
Investments: ($100,000)
Other Cashflows From Investing Activities: $0
Cash Flows From Investing Activities: ($184,025)

Cash Flow Financing Activities
Dividends Paid: $0
Sale Purchase of Stock: $359,875
Net Borrowings: ($121,968)
Other Cashflows From Financing Activities: $0
Cash Flows From Financing Activities: $237,907

Effect Of Exchange Rate: $0
Change In Cash And Cash Equivalents: ($616,364)

Finding Money To Pay For The Business

Raising Financing & $0-Down Strategies

The most commonly cited problem facing small business buyers is finding capital for the purchase. Most acquisitions are not successful because 99% of buyers looking for a business to buy do not have adequate financing to close on the transaction.

The reader needs to remember that taking control of the business is only one aspect of what creates the need for cash in an acquisition. Additional funds are also needed for:

- Closing cost, and

- Working capital

Closing Cost

Closing cost covers expenses such as lawyer and other professional fees, lease deposits for both utilities and rent, as well as various other expense items that will be encountered as the buyer goes through the process of buying the business. Remember that when the new owner takes control of the business, s/he will also have an obligation to assume utility bills and rent payments. Lease and utility deposits will be required and can add up to a considerable amount of money depending on the type of business being purchased. If the buyer's credit is not in excellent shape, there may be additional funds required by the utility companies and/or landlord before the transaction can close. Those expenses can amount to about 1% to 3% of the asking price of the business.

Working Capital

In addition to closing-related expenses mentioned above, there will be a need for working capital. When you transfer the assets of the business, there is generally no transfer of business funds from the company's coffers to the buyer. You take over the business with no capital in its bank account. The buyer needs to supply these funds to ensure that the business can meet its short-term operating expenses. The new owner needs to open a new checking account that will be used to deposit funds needed to pay employees and cover bills that will be due immediately after the closing. Depending on when the employees get paid, the buyer may be in need of several thousand dollars right after the closing.

To alleviate this financial burden, the buyer should consider one of the options described below.

Transfer of Working Capital at Closing

The buyer may be able (or try) to negotiate a price for the business that will help conserve some of the business' working capital as of a specified date. That is, the buyer might be able to convince the seller to transfer working capital as part of the business' assets transferred starting on an agreed-upon date. For example, it might be possible to negotiate with the seller to transfer all funds generated by the business as of the date you sign a "Letter of Intent." Of course that may mean the seller will want you to pay a little bit more for the business. But that will definitely help you solve an immediate cash crunch problem.

Decrease in Down Payment Amount

Another way to solve (or partially solve) such working capital and closing cost concerns is to negotiate a lower down payment with the seller. You might also be able to negotiate a "split" down payment. That is the buyer may ask the seller to partially finance the down payment and receive a portion at the closing and the other portion within a specified amount of time. Note, however, that this will drain the business' operating cash flow. Any time the buyer adds to the amount of leverage (or debt) that s/he uses in the purchase, there will be a need to somehow cut business expenses in order to make provisions to cover the additional debt

payments. Do not over-extend yourself!
Sometimes it may be wiser to simply not purchase a business, than to put a down payment and loose it because you can not meet your note payment. Remember that when you buy the business using debt (that is, you are leveraging the cash flow of the acquired business), the owner's attorney will make sure there is a guarantee of payment somewhere in the purchase contract. It might be your home if you own one, or it might be a lien on the business' assets themselves, such that if you are unable to make your payments, the business can be re-possessed.

Keeping The Seller's Security Deposits

In certain circumstances, the seller may agree to "lend" his/her security deposits to the buyer while s/he recovers from the acquisition. That is you may be able to take control of the business with no up-front cash to your new landlord and utility companies. It all depends on how convincing your proposal to the owner is, how well you negotiate your acquisition, and how motivated the seller is. Usually the seller will be more than happy to do that if there was a large enough down payment and you have the qualifications to run the business so that it will generate the additional cash to re-pay the deposits.

Sell or Borrow Against the Assets of the Business

This approach can only be used if the business has enough assets that you can dispose of some, and still produce enough cash to keep the business running without problems. These methods can also be used to finance the entire purchase. Among the many ways to do so, the following ones have been used by the author's clients:

- Sell or lease one location of a multi-location business. For example sell one location of a two-location gas station business, immediately after the acquisition, to retire some of the debt

- Finance the business' receivables, if applicable. Business owners can factor their receivables and receive reduced cash up front, instead of waiting for payment from their clients. The factoring company, basically buys your receivables for less than they are worth and collects from those who owe you, pocketing the difference

- Borrow against the assets of the business through an assets-based lender. If your business is asset-rich (e.g. a Laundromat), you can take a loan against these assets hopefully at a favorable rate (asset-based lenders usually charge very high interest rates on their loans), pay down some of your debt, and keep some of the cash to operate the new business. Some owners will even allow you to borrow against the machinery and equipment of the business in order to finance the purchase. This, of course, assumes that there is no prior loan outstanding against those assets.

Financing The Acquisition

Now that we've covered some possible ways to meet those closing costs and working capital requirements, let us discuss possible ways to finance the acquisition itself. We will leave out the conventional ways normally used when raising financing to purchase a business. We will not be discussing such financing channels as Venture Capital, Bank Financing, Savings, and Friends &

Family. Everyone knows that money can be raised through these channels, although it has proven extremely difficult for small business buyers to get bank or venture capital funding.

The only point we will make in that regard is that raising money from banks is many times easier when buying an operating business with good historical financial statements. If the buyer has extremely good credit, finding conventional money to buy a business, with the help of the Small Business Administration (SBA – www.sba.gov), is very simple. The buyer may have to guarantee the loan, maybe using his/her home as collateral. However some banks will even lend money for an acquisition without such loan guarantee. As long as the business has been operating for three years or more, and has a track record of profitability, the SBA is the easiest route to secure financing for the acquisition of a small company.

We will not launch into a discussion on how to write business plans to secure financing (a skeleton business plan is included in the Appendix), as this information can be obtained for free on the Internet. However, as a reference to the reader, we are including what we believe might be used to replace an actual business plan, as long as it is accompanied by the audited financials of the business that is being purchased. Such a profile, when presented to a lender can be used as a business plan because it presents a comprehensive synopsis of the business and its operations. If the banker or venture capitalist needs to see the details, s/he will ask for them. But in general, from our experience, if a business is going to get funded by a bank, "angel", or venture capital firm, such a profile will be enough to get the process started.

As a guideline, banks will lend you about 60% to 70% of the purchase price of business. The bank will probably require that you invest at least 10% of your own money in the venture, and you will generally not be allowed to borrow these additional funds from someone else. The Seller may finance the remaining balance. Venture Capital firms on the other hand will not require you to invest your own capital in the business. However, they will want you to have a great deal of experience in the type of business that you are buying. In addition, they will want to own part of the business with you, and you will generally not be free to do whatever you want while running the operation. For example, you may not be able to sell the business unless they give you permission to do so. Remember that they will be investing capital in your business and that will make them part owner, and hence will give them a voice when it comes to major decisions regarding the company.

Sample Business Profile For Acquisition Financing
(Present to lender with Audited Financials)

Business Highlights

- **Food (grocery) Delivery** and trucking company, servicing major accounts. This company is a private corporation with an established clientele and relationships, some of which in place since 1961
- **Key Delivery Points** include the following: Waldbaums, Key Foods, Krasdale, Shop Rite, Path Mark, A+P, White Rose
- **Highly Profitable** Business established in 1984 with **Offices** in New Jersey & Pennsylvania. Great growth potential
- **Machinery & Equipment** include: autos, tractors, shop equipment's and parts valued at $350,600
- **Property Description (Not included in Asking Price):** Truck parking for 25 trucks, Refueling capacity of 8,000 gallons, 5,000 sq. ft. of repair shop and 3,500 sq. ft. of office space
- **Location Description** Excellent location with own parking lot. Location is in a Business Park on a major highway in metro area of New Jersey with 200 ft of road frontage

- **Management & Employees.** Business is 100% owned by company President and has 13 <u>Non-Union</u> full-time employees. Owner is selling in order to facilitate company growth. Current employees will remain on board. **Employee breakdown:** *13* (all) drivers, *9* sales support/office staff
- **Major Nearby Attractions:** Teterboro Airport, Newark Airport, Kennedy Airport, and Conrail.
- **Large, currently un-used Warehouse** can also be part of this transaction. The warehouse is not being used at this time because the company lost the account when it became part of the Clorox Company through a recent merger

Locations Served: Northeast U.S.

- PA
- New York
- MA
- CT
- Rhode Island

Sample Business Profile for Acquisition Financing
(Present to lender or Venture Capital Firm with Audited Financials)

Three-Year Revenue Highlights ($)(000)

1998
  1,400
1999
  1,300
2000
  1,450

Summary Financials ($)

Major Expenses *(Yearly Amount)*
Payroll (excluding owner): $572,000
Payroll taxes: $72,000
Insurance: $75,000
Rent: $54,000
Real Estate Taxes: $8,000
Utilities: $7,200
Equipment Lease: $662
Total Yearly Expense: $788,862

Equipment & Assets Value *(included in Price)*
Autos & Tractors: $300,800
Shop Equipment: $15,000
Parts: $34,800

Total: $350,600

Transaction Summary

- Asking Price: $1.1 million
- Asking price includes inventory, machinery & equipment. Real estate is not included in the Asking Price. Seller will negotiate leasing of the facility with the buyer
---

Now let us assume that a buyer does not have good credit and/or does not have part, or all the funds necessary to acquire the business. We can only recommend the following two ways to help complete the transaction:

- Owner Financing
- Lease-To-Own with Owner Financing

Both methods require a lot of patience and a very motivated seller. However, we first need to clarify one important point. No one can buy a business if s/he does not have any source of financing. Whether those funds are from the buyer's bank account, credit card loans, lines of credit from financial institutions, a loan from the seller, there must be a source of money to be able to carry out the purchase of a business. There is really no such thing as a "real" no-money-down transaction. The funds for the acquisition may not be the buyer's, but money is always needed to buy a small business.

A seller may be very motivated because s/he has to move and desperately needs to sell the business. That seller may agree to sell the business to a buyer with no money down, but it is certain that there will be some contingencies, which will require the buyer to come up with some cash. For example, s/he may ask you to pay the lawyer's fees. Another scenario might be that the seller has to pay a small debt if the business is sold. You may be able to assume the debt. However, if the creditor does not approve your assumption of the loan, you may have to pay a lump sum on that debt before being able to refinance it.

Option 1: Owner Financing

Owner financing is one of the easiest ways to finance the acquisition of a business if i) the buyer has some cash for a down payment; and ii) there is a motivated seller. In a seller-financed purchase, the seller in essence becomes the bank. You pay him or her a down payment and sign a promissory note that you will pay the balance of that loan from the business' cash flow at an agreed upon interest rate and length of time.

     Usually the down payment is due at closing and the first payment on the note, one month after the closing. However, you may be able to negotiate with the seller on a different starting date for debt re-payment. If you had a large enough initial down payment, you may be able to negotiate a grace period like in a real estate purchase. To secure the debt, the owner will most likely put a lien against the assets of the business. Some owners may require the buyer to put a lien on their personal residence, depending on the type and profitability of the business. The key here is the buyer's negotiation skills and experience in the field. A schedule of payments is shown below based on a $100,000 asking price with a 20% down payment to the owner. The balance is due over 5 years at a rate of 5%.

Table 18 Sample Owner Financing Business Loan Analysis

Amount financed: $80,000.00
Annual interest (e.g., 8.25): 5.000
Duration of loan (in years): 5
Monthly payments: $1,509.70
Total number of payments: 60
Yearly principal + interest: $18,116.38
Principal amount: $80,000.00
Finance charges: $10,581.92
Total cost: $90,581.92

Beginning Balance: $80,000.00
Interest: $333.33
Principal: $1,176.37
Balance: $78,823.63
Interest: $333.33
Principal: $1,176.37

Beginning Balance: $78,823.63
Interest: $328.43
Principal: $1,181.27
Balance: $77,642.37
Interest: $661.77
Principal: $2,357.63

Beginning Balance: $77,642.37

Interest: $323.51
Principal: $1,186.19
Balance: $76,456.18
Interest: $985.28
Principal: $3,543.82

Beginning Balance: $76,456.18
Interest: $318.57
Principal: $1,191.13
Balance: $75,265.05
Interest: $1,303.84
Principal: $4,734.95

Beginning Balance: $75,265.05
Interest: $313.60
Principal: $1,196.09
Balance: $74,068.95
Interest: $1,617.45
Principal: $5,931.05

Beginning Balance: $74,068.95
Interest: $308.62
Principal: $1,201.08
Balance: $72,867.88
Interest: $1,926.07
Principal: $7,132.12

Option 2: Lease-To-Own with Owner Financing

This is an option that is harder to come around as sellers would sometimes hold on to their business and hire a manager to operate it for them instead, if they are not able to run it themselves. The circumstances of such a sale will be the key points in closing on this transaction. Furthermore, the seller should not be selling because there is an immediate need for cash.

Basically in this case, you are simply purchasing the business under the same scenario discussed above. However, you are adding a leasing period to it prior to the closing, before actually transferring the assets. In addition, the down payment is not due to the owner until the closing (after the leasing period), although payments to the owner are scheduled on a monthly basis, as if the down payment had been paid at the beginning of the leasing period.

However, there has to be something for the seller in the transaction as s/he is giving you the right to operate and manage the business for the entire agreed-upon leasing period. During that period, you are basically benefiting from the operating cash flow without actually owning the business. In the process, the potential buyer is also building a cash reserve. The only way to make this offer valuable to the seller, if s/he is even willing to consider it (the author actually worked on such a transaction), is to guarantee that if you do not purchase the business after the leasing period, any money gained during that leasing period will be fully reimbursed. This means that if during the leasing period, after all business operating expenses and note payments to the seller, any funds were retained as profits, such funds should be returned to the seller. A more attractive approach might be to park the additional funds in an escrow account to be returned to the seller, in the event that the transaction does not go through.

This scenario can also be used by someone who actually has the down payment, but wishes to "test-drive" the business before buying it. In that case, the down payment can be put in escrow for the entire leasing period.

A sample payment structure follows for such a purchase. Note that the closing happens after the leasing period, when the down payment is disbursed to the seller, although monthly note payments to the seller are paid out as if the down payment had already been received. It is also important to realize that this leasing period can be used by a buyer who has a portion of the down payment and wants to raise the balance by actually working for the seller before the closing.

A schedule of payments is shown below based on a $100,000 asking price and a 20% post-leasing down payment to the owner. The balance is due over five years at a rate of 5%. In such a case, the first monthly payment is paid at the beginning of the leasing period. In this scenario, the leasing period is to last for 3 months. (Note the $20,000 balloon Principal payment that is added to the regular monthly payment on the 4th month, after the leasing period)

Table 19 Sample Owner Financing Business Loan Analysis – Lease To Own

Amount financed: $80,000.00
Annual interest (e.g., 8.25): 5.000
Duration of loan (in years): 5
Monthly payments: $1,509.70
Total number of payments: 60
Yearly principal + interest: $18,116.38
Principal amount: $80,000.00
Finance charges: $10,581.92
Total cost: $90,581.92

Beginning Balance: $80,000.00
Interest: $333.33
Principal: $1,176.37
Balance: $78,823.63
Interest: $333.33
Principal: $1,176.37

Beginning Balance: $78,823.63
Interest: $328.43
Principal: $1,181.27
Balance: $77,642.37
Interest: $661.77
Principal: $2,357.63

Beginning Balance: $77,642.37

Interest: $323.51
Principal: $1,186.19
Balance: $76,456.18
Interest: $985.28
Principal: $3,543.82

Beginning Balance: $76,456.18
Interest: $318.57
Principal: $21,191.13 (Lump Sum Payment)
Balance: $75,265.05
Interest: $1,303.84
Principal: $4,734.95

Beginning Balance: $75,265.05
Interest: $313.60
Principal: $1,196.09
Balance: $74,068.95
Interest: $1,617.45
Principal: $5,931.05

Beginning Balance: $74,068.95
Interest: $308.62
Principal: $1,201.08
Balance: $72,867.88
Interest: $1,926.07
Principal: $7,132.12

Special Financing Section: An Unconventional Source Of Capital

We would like to end this section by briefly talking about a very unusual approach often used to raise short-term capital in the Caribbean. This is a method mostly used to save money for special events, such as the purchase of a car. It has become so popular in the US now, that banks use it as an acceptable way to finance the down payment for the purchase of a home. We believe that in certain circumstances, it might be a great capital formation strategy for a small business buyer.

The following are the most important characteristics of this technique:

- It is initiated by a Group of five (5) or more people

- Each member of the Group is employed or is a business owner

- The Group is supervised by a manager (usually the organizing member)

- There is a solid commitment by all members to carry out the entire "round" (to be discussed shortly)

- Group members are required to contribute an affordable monthly (or whatever contribution frequency they agree upon) amount, usually $500 or more

To carry out the task of helping its members raise needed capital, a Group can be defined by the following:

- Number of members

- Group head: the person in charge of collecting contributions and disbursements to members. This person is also responsible for keeping track of the logistics of the Group. That is, s/he keeps track of members that have received their round, those that are missing contributions, etc.

- Contribution amount

- Frequency of contribution (usually monthly)

Such a Group is basically a twisted version of an investment club. Members, usually friends and/or family, unless there is an independent Group

Manager, agree to pool money by contributing monthly to the fund. Each month, one member gets the entire amount contributed by all members in a round robin fashion. The cycle continues until everyone has received a pay-out, also called a "take" or hand.

Note that this is simply a way to get a lump sum at a specific time based on your position in the queue. For a business buyer, the best position in the queue is probably the first one, because the first person in the queue receives the first "take". This would then allow for his/her future contributions to be drawn from the operations of the acquired business. Please note that this is not a savings account. In the end, contributions and pay-outs cancel each other, such that members do not gain or loose any money at the end of a round. (See table below). In addition, money contributed by the Group's members is never deposited in a bank account, hence earns no interest.

To illustrate, let us create a fictitious Group of three members (Member 1, Member 2, and Member 3), with a contribution amount of $100 due weekly. There are as many cycles (or rounds) as there are members, in this case three cycles (Week 1, Week 2, Week 3). The total amount of each member's take when his/her turn arrives is $300, which is also equal to the total amount of money contributed.

Table 20 Sample Pooling Group Contribution & Pay-out Table

Week 1

--Member 1
Contribution: $100
Pay Out: **$300**

--Member 2
Contribution: $100
Pay Out: Not applicable

--Member 3
Contribution: $100
Pay Out: Not applicable

Week 2

--Member 1
Contribution: $100
Pay Out: Not applicable

--Member 2
Contribution: $100
Pay Out: **$300**

--Member 3
Contribution: $100
Pay Out: Not applicable

Week 3

--Member 1
Contribution: $100
Pay Out: Not applicable

--Member 2
Contribution: $100
Pay Out: Not applicable

--Member 3
Contribution: $100
Pay Out: **$300**

So, if a buyer can manage to create one of these Pooling Groups around the time that the closing is scheduled to take place, s/he can use this very simple technique to raise the necessary funds to close on an acquisition.

Legal and Tax Issues

Acquisition Options

Overview

Although many legal and tax issues are at play when a business is being purchased, we will not go into the details of all that can be involved. This is only because the author assumes that the reader will be engaged in a simple transaction in which the tax and legal implications are not so complex that they make these issues ground for concerns. We are also assuming that the buyer will use the services of a lawyer to effectively complete the purchase and close on the transaction. No one would think of buying real estate without a lawyer. The same should apply to buying a business, where transfer of real estate assets may be involved.

Assets vs. Stock Purchase

The most important aspect of an acquisition when small businesses are concerned, is whether the buyer will be acquiring the stock of the business, or its assets.

To make this clear, let us define a business (which we will assume is a small corporation) as a collection of assets and liabilities. Assets can be real estate, cash, contracts, receivables, equipment and machinery. Liabilities, of course, are what the business owes to its creditors, shareholders and stakeholders (such as employees). Those can be bank loans, back taxes, payroll, etc.

When a buyer completes an acquisition through a stock purchase, that buyer inherits everything that makes up the business, both assets and liabilities. If a buyer simply wants to take over the assets, it has to be specified in the Letter of Intent that the transaction will be structured as an asset purchase, instead of a stock purchase, which means that the buyer will not be responsible for the company's liabilities once the business has been acquired. Those liabilities not assumed, and which may include bank loans, among other debts, will continue to be the responsibility of the seller, even after the business has been sold.

Stock sales are often used when the seller is financing the transaction under such conditions that the buyer will assume the company's debts. However, if a buyer has some portion of the down payment and has obtained bank financing, there is no need to assume company debt, unless the asking price is reduced to reflect the assumed liability. However, if a buyer has agreed to acquire the liabilities of a business as well as its assets in a stock purchase, the Due Diligence process should be even more extensive in order to ensure that the new owner totally understands what is involved in the transaction and the extent of the debt that s/he is assuming.

Running The Business

A Quick Guide For The New Owner

      This book is not about running a business. Several good books have been written about the subject. Accordingly, this section will be very short, as we simply want to quickly review what we believe are three of the most important aspects of running a small business. In order words, we want to help keep the new owner on high alert with respect to the following issues:

- Hiring and keeping good employees, and firing the bad ones,

- Managing the business' finances, and

- Keeping customers happy

Hiring and Keeping Good Employees

Buying a business helps alleviate the human resources problems of a new owner. The business is normally purchased as a running concern with employees, unless the seller was the only employee. Keeping employees is not an easy task as problems arise constantly and personalities clash. The key driver in nurturing good relationships with employees is to treat them fairly. To do that, it is important to do some research. The most important one, we believe, is to at least find out how much your competitors are paying their employees for similar jobs and work conditions. Then it is in the new owner's best interest to "match" that salary.

Of course a small business owner may not be able to afford to pay its employees what a larger competitor is paying. However, the difference in salary can be made up with special perks (for example paid lunch one or two days of the week), added responsibility, a small bonus when jobs are performed exceptionally, etc. There are many ways to make employees happy and it is up to the owner to be as creative as it is needed. The bottom line is that employees can only be happy with their job if they:

- Like what they do,

- Are paid well for what they do, and

- Are challenged and respected

However, it is important to note that it will be impossible to please everyone. Many (if not all) employees hired by a small business are simply "killing" time until the ideal job is found somewhere else. So do not take it personally when things do not work out with an employee, even after the owner has spent the time and money to accommodate that employee's needs.

In addition, at times it will be necessary to let an employee go. That makes an Employee Procedures Manual a must. That will help avoid the legal complications that may arise when an employee is fired. This manual will have to be written in a very clear manner. It will also need to outline you business' Rules and Regulations, which if broken, will be ground for letting an employee go. Finally, keep a log of everything that happens in your business. Document every conversation you have had with an employee who was not meeting your performance quota, or was not behaving properly.

Managing Business Finances

No buyer is thinking about meeting payroll when s/he is closing on a newly acquired business. The excitement of being one's own boss can certainly be a blinding experience.

However, especially, in the case of a small business which was bought using all kinds of credit cards and owner financing options, there is often horrific times waiting ahead. A business that is purchased using a lot of debt can become a great burden if the owner is not prepared. There will be lots of bills to pay at the beginning of the month following the closing. Until then, employees have to be paid and operating expenses have to be funded.

In order to avoid the embarrassment of having checks of your employees and creditors bounce, not to mention the bank fees associated with that, we would recommend taking the following steps:

- Immediately (within the first 2 days) upon taking possession of the business, run a complete analysis of current expenses. Without impairing the operations, cut all unnecessary outlays of cash

- Do a thorough due diligence on how to increase your sales. From flyer distribution to hiring commissioned sales people, by any means, increase your revenue stream

- Delay or cancel all big purchases, unless it is critical to business operations

- If not already in place, start paying your employees every other week, instead of once a week, in order to improve your operating cash flow

- Do a complete review of your staff, if applicable. Let go of anyone whose workload could be spread among other employees without too much damage, and without hindering the work of those employees

- Try your best to re-negotiate with your landlord. Is it possible to pay no rent for a month or two? If not, would your landlord accept half of your rent payment for a month or two? Some landlords will give as much as six months worth of free rent to a new tenant, depending on the tenant's credit, line of business, and length of lease

- For as long as possible, the new owner should not withdraw any salary from the business until it is clear that there will be enough cash from the operations to support the business and pay the bills

Our advice is never to wait until the last minute to start finding ways to increase your cash flow. The most embarrassing thing that can happen to a small business owner is to have employees unable to cash their checks because there is not sufficient funds in the business' checking account. This can destroy your reputation because words will travel fast and that will impair your ability to hire good employees and get credit from suppliers.

Keeping Customers Happy

The best way to keep customers happy is to keep employees happy, assuming that the employees have been trained properly to meet the customers' needs. Having said that, we believe there are still ways, independent of employee satisfaction, to keep your customers coming back. Some franchisers actually charge their franchisees a fee for not keeping their clients happy, because customers are the lifeblood of a business and the entire organization's goal should be to satisfy those customers' needs. What follows should simply be used as food for thoughts. They have proven very useful in running the author's own businesses.

A. Hours of Operations and Convenience

Convenience is what customers are looking for, and a business can certainly use it to differentiate itself from its competitors. To take an example from the car rental industry, most small neighborhood car renal businesses require that on Fridays, a customer rent a car for the entire weekend. It makes sense for the business owner, but most of the time that doesn't make any sense at all for the customer who may simply need the car for a Saturday morning meeting. Why pay for three days when you only need the car for half a day? The author's and his wife's car rental business opens seven days a week and does not require customers who rent on Friday to keep the car for three days. This has resulted in a flux of clients from neighboring boroughs. A business owner's job is to pay attention to all the details that can help make life more convenient for the customers.

B. Pricing and Discounts

Although most customers would choose convenience over price, the majority of customers will mention price if they believe, or have found out, that a business is charging more than its surrounding competitors. For that reason, we suggest that business owners periodically "survey" their competitors' prices and adjust theirs accordingly. This does not mean a business should always sell its products or services at the lowest prices. Usually customers will be willing to pay more when good customer service accompanies a good product or service. Putting your price in line with that of your competitors simply guarantees that your customers will come back to you.

C. Product Knowledge

Nothing is more frustrating than getting the wrong answers from someone who should know the right answers. Giving your customers false or incorrect information may cost you money. It is basically unacceptable to provide inaccurate information to someone who does business with you and your employees. The customer would prefer that you honestly admit that you do not know the answer, with a promise to research it. The key remedy for such a problem is training. The new owner has to ensure that all new (and current) employees have a thorough knowledge of all products and services the business provide to its customers. Product knowledge will bring customers back because customers always have questions and problems (which is the reason why they come to you in the first place). Being an expert at what you do will convey confidence to your customers who will simply not even think of going anywhere else. This, in fact, is why large companies such as Home Depot are now offering free classes to their clients.

Epilogue

Buying a business is hard work, not to mention the risk of possibly failing and loosing all your invested savings. However, with patience and by following the steps outlined in this book, a potential buyer can become the owner of a successful operating business. As the reader might know, buying an existing business with a history of profit, even small, puts the owner in a better position for success. Research has shown that startup businesses are very likely to fail within the first three years. Whereas buying a business that is operating successfully is more likely to continue to operate successfully, unless the new owner is so inexperienced that s/he drives the business to the ground.

Our section on Due Diligence can however help the buyer to avoid such catastrophe. The buyer should make sure that s/he executes a thorough Due Diligence on the target business, or businesses. Follow the guidelines outlined in this book to determine the value of your potential acquisition. This will ensure that the appropriate price is paid for a business that will not go under once control has been transferred.

The prospective buyer's ultimate goal is to buy a small business that will produce enough cash to fuel the operations of the business, support the new owner, and still have additional funds to allow for a possible expansion either internally or through acquisitions. If the target business is barely breaking even, or loosing money, do not purchase it, regardless of the terms.

Finally make sure not to over-leverage an acquisition. Too much debt can result in a business failing once it has changed hands because the owner is not able to meet his/her debt payments. The rule of thumb is that the business should be able to pay for operating expenses, cover debt payment, support the owner and still have excess cash (even a very small amount) left for emergencies and/or expansion.

About RGL Learning

RGL Learning is a small Training and Publishing company whose mission is to publish educational books and eBooks, and to provide online training to the Small Business market. Please visit our web site at http://rgllearning.com or contact us at info@rgllearning.com.

About Rudy LeCorps

The author and his wife are the owners of various businesses, including a Car Rental Franchise and a Training & Publishing company, located in Northern New Jersey and New York City.

Appendix & Additional Resources and Case Study

No-Money-Down Acquisition Case Study

What follows is the Term Sheet (another name used to refer to a Letter of Intent) of an actual acquisition in which the author was involved. This was a transaction in which a publicly traded school holding company was buying a small chain of technology training schools with locations in New Jersey, New York, Canada and China. Due diligence followed immediately after the Term Sheet was signed by the seller. Names and addresses have been omitted for confidentiality purposes.

Definitive Term Sheet Dated July 10, 2001

Outline of Business Terms for the Acquisition of [Company Division I] (NY); [Company Division II] (New Jersey) Inc.; [Company Division III] (Canada), Inc. (Operating as [Company Name] Computer Institute); and [Company Division IV], Inc. China (including any interests held by [Owner's Name] or other shareholders collectively hereinafter referred to as "[Company Name]") by [Buyer's Company Name], Inc. or its designated subsidiary (hereinafter referred to as Buyer)

1. Seller agrees that, at the Closing, it will sell, assign, transfer, and deliver all of its interests in [Seller] including without limitation any [Seller Name] common or preferred shares, options, warrants, and any debt instruments and all other interests held by Sellers, free and clear of any

Encumbrance, and Buyer agrees that it will purchase such interests.
2. The Buyer hereby agrees that the Purchase Price shall be paid and satisfied by the Buyer as follows:
   A. Warrants to purchase 350,000 shares of [Buying Company] Common Stock at a strike price of 110% of the 10 day average closing offer price for the ten days prior to the closing, but in no event less than $1.00 per share.
   B. [Selling Company's Owner's Name] shall receive a contract entitling him to receive $300,000 per year for 4 years or until he receives a total of $1 million within the same four year period. Of the yearly amount specified herein, $100,000 shall be paid for consulting services and up to $200,000 per year shall be paid from an amount equal to 20% of the free cash flow of [Selling Company Name]. In addition, Mr. [Selling Company's Owner's Name] may act as a nonexclusive recruitment and referral agent for Asian students wishing to study at any [Buyer] subsidiary post-secondary institution. Such subsidiary, after collecting all tuition and fees for foreign students referred to an [Buyer] subsidiary and

recruited by Mr. [Selling Company's Owner's Name] and admitted to such [Buyer] subsidiary, shall pay to Mr. [Selling Company's Owner's Name] 20% of all tuition and fees generated and collected from such students.
3. Seller's key Executive I and Seller's key Executive II shall each sign an employment contract with [Selling Company] at the date of closing for a term of 1 year with renewal options thereafter.
4. [Selling Company] must provide 3 years of Audited Financial Statements for each school for the years ending December 31, 2000 in accordance with US GAAP and shall provide a "stub audit" for that part of the year 2001 that is appropriate under SEC requirements, given the targeted closing date.
5. Present management may designate one board member to the [Selling Company] Board of Directors
6. All governmental and regulatory approvals and all consents of third parties (including for example certification agencies and landlords), and compliance with any conditions thereof, required in connection with the completion of any of the transactions contemplated by the definitive Agreement, the closing or the

performance of any of the terms and conditions set forth in the definitive Agreement shall have been obtained and complied with on or before the Closing.
7. [Selling Company's Owner's Name] has represented that a $500,000 line of credit is available to [Selling Company] and that he has personally guaranteed such credit facility. As a condition of the closing, [Selling Company's Owner's Name] shall keep such line of credit in place. In return, [Buying Company] shall provide to [Selling Company's Owner's Name] a full and unconditional indemnity, with a right of subrogation in favor of [Buying Company], and in form and substance reasonably satisfactory to [Selling Company's Owner's Name], to hold harmless [Selling Company's Owner's Name] against any claim, demand, action, cause of action, damages, loss, cost, liability or expense which may be made or brought against [Selling Company's Owner's Name] as a result of or arising out of such line of credit. Such obligation to indemnify [Selling Company's Owner's Name] shall be limited to the aggregate amount of $500,000.
8. The definitive agreement shall incorporate an appropriate non-compete section prohibiting [Selling Company's Owner's Name] from

engaging in, directly or indirectly, any company which in any way is competing with [Selling Company] within a 100-mile radius of [Selling Company] or any of its branches or extensions wherever located.
9. The parties shall do all things and provide all reasonable assurances as may be required to consummate the transactions contemplated by this term sheet and each party shall provide such further documents or instruments required by any other party as may be reasonably necessary or desirable to effect the purposes of this Term Sheet.
10. Parties recognize that Finder's Fees for introducing the parties are due by [Selling Company] to [Broker] and by [Buying Company] to [Selling Company's Advisor] Each party shall have the responsibility to compensate their own Finders.
11. This Agreement shall be governed and construed in accordance with the laws of the State of New York.

In witness whereof the parties have hereunto duly executed this Agreement on the date first above written.

       [Buying Company Name]
By_____

Separately list each [Selling Company's Division] Corporation shown above

End of Definitive Term Sheet

Valuation Resources on the Internet

Web Site/
Description

moneysoft.com/
MoneySoft provides structured and intelligent software systems for making sound, prudent business decisions in the areas of corporate acquisitions, business valuation and fixed asset management.

nvst.com/
The Private Equity Network® is a meeting place for Investors, Advisors, and Entrepreneurs of privately held businesses.

due.com/
Due.Com is a proprietary, technology-based Intelligent Due Diligence™ (IDD) information system

SBA List of S.B.I.C.s (Small Business Investment Corporation)

http://www.sba.gov/gopher/Local-Information/Small-Business-Investment-Companies/

The web address above has been retrieved from the Small Business Administration's (S.B.A.) web site and contains a comprehensive list of S.B.I.C.s by state. Information about each firm includes type and size (in dollars) of investment in a small business, as well as contact name and address to forward business plans and investment proposals.

Skeleton Business Plan

Section/
Description

Executive Summary
An overview of what the business is about, including a brief summary of its financials such as projected sales and income, as well as the amount of capital being sought

---

Objectives
The objective the buyer wants to achieve by buying the business

---

Mission
The mission statement of the business being acquired

Keys to Success
Most important elements to achieving success in the business and industry

---

Market Analysis (Text)
Analysis of the market in which the business is being acquired. This usually includes outlook for the industry, growth trend, barrier to entry, etc.

Market Analysis (Table)
Any information related to Market Analysis that can be presented in table form belongs in this section

---

Market Analysis (Chart)
Market analysis information is usually more convincing when presented with charts as the reader of the plan can easily scan for trends, increases and decreases in past and projected numbers

---

Break-even (Tables)
This will most likely not apply to an existing business unless it is being purchased as a turnaround opportunity and is currently loosing money

---

Break-even (Charts)
Again, use charts every time possible to as it is easier for the business plan reader to see in which direction your business is moving

---

Conclusion
Basically a summary of the business plan

Sample Executive Summary

The Executive Summary plays a major role in helping a business buyer attract financing because it is the first section that commercial bankers and venture capitalists review when analyzing investment opportunities. It is actually recommended that when submitting proposals for financing, the prospective buyer initially submit only the Executive Summary. If enough interest is raised from that summary, s/he will be asked to submit the entire business plan. To help the reader, we are including a sample Executive Summary, which can be modified and inserted into a business plan. This summary was extracted from the business plan of a Buyout Fund (SBBF) which was a partnership established to buy other small businesses.

----SAMPLE EXECUTIVE SUMMARY-------

OVERVIEW

This executive summary is for the proposed creation of a Small Business Buyout Fund (hereafter called SBBF). The Fund's mission will be to provide a greatly needed service for small business owners who sell or liquidate their businesses: an **Exit Point**, in essence establishing a platform that will create a small Market for selected small businesses.

Unlike a Venture Capital fund, SBBF will not be taking partial equity stakes in target businesses or invest in startups. The Fund's goal is to acquire and own small operating businesses.

Like a Buyout Fund, the proposed fund will buy businesses directly from the owners and hire experienced managers to run them if the owners decide to leave. Unlike a normal Buyout Fund, SBBF will use its funds to acquire small, privately held businesses valued at $2.5MM or less. Initially emphasis will be placed on businesses located in New York and New Jersey.

Like large Buyout Funds, SBBF will use leverage to make the most of available capital. Unlike those funds, SBBF will not use bank or public debts for its acquisitions. Leverage will be in the form of promissory Notes to the Sellers, thereby creating a debt due to those sellers.

We are proposing a debt ratio of 4 to 1. That is 25% of the sale price will be paid in cash to the seller as a down payment at closing. The balance will be due over time at an agreed upon interest rate and length, which will depend on the type and profitability of the business.

In order to create such a fund, we are asking selected investors (including certain large Private Equity and Buyout Funds) for **Equity Investments, or Investment Commitments totaling $25 million**. Such an amount will have a total buying power of $100 million, based on a ratio of 4 to 1. That, in turn, will allow us to take advantage of an opportunity, which we believe can create yearly returns of as much as 50% on investors' capital in any economic environment, depending on how discounted acquisitions are, and how much value can be added to acquired businesses through operating improvements. However, our experience working with small businesses has proven that a pool of motivated sellers is out there waiting for buyers.

THE OPPORTUNITY
According to the U.S. Chamber of Commerce, small businesses:
- Represent over 99% of all employer firms,
- Employ 52% of all private workers,
- Account for 51% of the private sector output, and
- Are responsible for virtually all new jobs through creation of new firms as well as expansion of existing small businesses.

The Chamber goes on to report that approximately one in five privately owned businesses (20%) experiences change of ownership during any particular year, which results in the transfer of ownership involving more than two million businesses yearly. It is also good to note that the average sale price of a small business is around $200,000.

This creates a multi-billion dollar market that has been totally ignored by the large Buyout and Private Equity firms. SBBF's goal is to capture that opportunity and create sizable returns for its investors by:

- Using an owner-financing model of purchase,
- Bringing immediate cash to the table for down payments, and
- Facilitating discounted acquisitions

BUSINESS MODEL
We are proposing a fund that will generate revenues and create value for its investors by:

- Always buying businesses at a discount using its buying power of available cash
  The biggest problem for an owner selling a small business is to find a buyer who has the down payment to close on the transaction. 99% of transactions in the small business market don't close because of lack of financing, even when sellers are willing to hold notes
- Improving operations, thereby increasing the value of the businesses acquired as well as their profit margin
- Re-selling businesses for their full price, or a premium, after a 3 to 5 year holding period

ORGANIZATIONAL STRUCTURE
We are proposing to establish a governing board of seven (7) members whose responsibility will be to:

- Review acquisitions targets submitted by the Fund's finder (see below) and make purchase decisions,
- Hire qualified managers to run the businesses, if the owners decide to leave,
- Decide when businesses are sold, and
- Report the Fund's progress to investors on a quarterly basis

Currently 1 board member has been identified (the other 6 are to be designated by the Fund's investors):

(a) **[Board Member Name]**
    [Board Member background]

FUND MANAGEMENT & FEE

There will be no management fee. However, for services rendered as a full-time finder for the Fund, we are simply asking for a 5% ownership share in each business acquired.

Our services to the Fund will be comprehensive and include (but not limited to) the following duties and activities:

- Comprehensive and methodical search for businesses that meet the Fund's acquisition criteria

- Packaging of target acquisitions. All relevant information about each business identified for purchase will be assembled and compiled into an "Acquisition Data Packet" and presented to the board for consideration
- Extensive Due Diligence and Valuation Analysis of all businesses approved by the Board for possible acquisition
- Mediation between the Board and the target business' owner and his / her advisors
- Search for managers for the Board to interview when the owner of an acquisition will not stay to run it
- Intermediary between each acquisition's manager and the Board
- Identification of possible buyers for acquisitions that the Board has decided to sell

<u>INDUSTRY FOCUS</u>
We are proposing that SBBF focus its funds into the sectors listed below. According to the U.S. Chamber of Commerce, as well as our experience in the Small Business Market, these segments have proven to be the fastest growing small-business dominated industries:

- Restaurants
- Trucking, Transportation & Storage
- Outpatient Care Facilities & Physician Offices
- Supermarkets
- Special Trade Construction Contractors
- Computer & Data Processing Services, including Computer Schools and Training Centers
- Medical & Dental Laboratories
- Day Care Services

POSSIBLE SCENARIO FOR AN OPPORTUNISTIC ACQUISITION

What follows describes one scenario where SBBF could achieve above average returns through the discounted purchase of a small business. In this scenario, we use numbers that we believe might represent an average for all transactions completed.

Summary Financials

Yearly Revenue: $3,920,000
Total Expenses:$3,528,000
Net Income: $392,000
Market value (a): $980,000
Margin(%): 10

Acquisition Structure

Discount (%): 8
Purchase Price: $901,600
Down Payment (b): $225,400

Debt Payment (c)

Balance Due to Owner: $676,200
Monthly Payment: $8,681
Yearly Debt Amount (f): $104,169

Yearly Return Analysis (d)

Net Income minus Debt: $287,831
Total Return (%)(e): 78

Notes:

1. Our Market Value is based on a straight multiple (2.5x) of Net Income.

2. Down Payment is equal to 25% of negotiated purchase price of $901,600, which yields an 8% discount on the value of the business.
3. Debt Payment is based on a 5-year repayment schedule at the rate of 5%.
4. Our Return Analysis is assuming that the business will continue to run as is with no improvement in operations. Total debt payment is taken off the Net Income for an adjusted Net Income of $287,831. That number in turn, when divided into the actual money invested in the business – down payment amount of $225,400 – results in a Total Return of 78%.
5. That amount is not taking into account that the Fund may have to add working capital into the business in addition to the down payment.
6. Note that at such a rate, if the business were to be held for the entire 5-year loan period, the owner would actually receive $816,686, in addition to the down payment. That would exceed the $980,000 estimated value of the business.

CLOSING WORDS

Thousands of small businesses are for sale each day. The majority of those businesses cannot be sold and have been on the market for 9 months or more because the buyers do not have the necessary financing to complete the purchase, even when the sellers are willing to sell at a discount and hold note.

With a Small Business Buyout Fund as proposed in this document, acquisitions will be extremely opportunistic because of the availability of cash for a down payment. This will create a tremendous buying power that will allow us to:

- Serve small business owners who do not have a public market to harvest the fruit of their work, and
- Create generous returns for our investors

Contact Information
[Contact Information Here]

===================================
End of Sample Executive Summary
===================================

Glossary

Acquisition Loans: Debt used to finance the purchase of a business

Annuity or Pay Out: A series of regular consecutive payments or receipts of equal amount

Appraisal: A professional opinion of the value of a business or other property

Asset-based Analysis: Valuation methodology that uses the fair market value, rather than the book value, of items on a company's balance sheet.

Asset Purchase: A type of transaction in which the buyer purchases assets from the target company, rather than a Stock Purchase in which the buyer purchases the shares of the target company

Auction: A sale that is intended to be accomplished by a process of requesting Bids on a business by a specified date

Balance Sheet: A financial statement that includes the company's assets, liabilities, and equity as of a particular date.

Bankruptcy: The state of being unable to pay debts when due and having then filed with a court seeking the reorganization or Liquidation of a company.

Bid: This is the stated price a buyer is willing to pay for an asset or a business.

Book Value: A company's book value is its total assets minus intangible assets and liabilities, such as debt. A company's book value might be more or less than its Market Value. Also known as Net Worth.

Break-even Analysis: An analysis of the sales level at which a project would make zero profit. The break-even point can be computed by dividing Fixed Costs by product price minus Variable Cost per product unit.

Business Broker: Professional who assists in arranging the purchase, sale, or financing of a business

Capital Markets: A place or system in which the requirements for the capital needed in a business can be obtained.

Capitalization of Earning Power Method: A method of determining the value of a business by dividing a company's earnings by a certain Discount Rate or Required Rate of Return.

Cash Flow Lenders: Financial institutions that lend money primarily based on a company's ability to generate cash flow to service the debt.

Commercial Paper: Short-term unsecured promissory note.

Common Stockholder: A holder of common stock (or share) of a company.

Comparable Transaction Analysis: A market-based valuation methodology in which the sale transactions of similar companies are analyzed.

Confidentiality Agreement: See Non-Disclosure Agreement.

Consolidation: The combining of two or more companies to form an entirely new entity.

Cost of Capital: The cost of alternative sources of financing for a company.

Cost of Goods Sold (COGS): The total cost of buying raw materials, and for all of the factors that go directly into producing finished goods. Or, in the case of a service business, the direct cost of delivering the service.

Current Assets: All of a company's assets that can be converted to cash within one-year, typically includes cash, cash equivalents, accounts receivables, inventory, marketable securities, and prepaid expenses.

Current Liabilities: All of a company's debts that are due within one year, typically includes accounts payable and accrued liabilities

Deal Structure: The manner in which a transaction is structured.

Debt Ratios: Ratios that indicate the extent to which debt is being used and how it relates to a company's operations. A high ratio indicates higher risks and perhaps higher returns.

Discount Rate: The rate used to determine the present value of a stream of future cash flow.

Discounted Cash Flow (DCF) Analysis: A valuation method in which the sum of the present value of a company's future free cash flows is equal to the fair market value of a business.

Dividend: The portion of a company's profit paid to Shareholders.

Due Diligence: The review by the acquirer of a target company's internal books and operations. Transactions are often made contingent upon the result of the due diligence.

Earn Out: A contractual provision enabling an owner to earn additional money after the sale of a business if certain conditions are met.

Earnings Before Interest, Taxes, Depreciation, and Amortization (EBITDA): A financial measure defined as revenues less cost of goods sold and selling, general, and administrative expenses.

Fair Market Value: The aggregate price at which a business would change hands between a willing buyer and a willing seller.

Financial Leverage: The use of debt to increase the expected Return on an acquisition.

Financial Ratios: The result of dividing one financial statement item by another.

Fixed Costs: A cost that is fixed for a given period of time, regardless of production levels.

Free Cash Flow: The various cash flow streams that may be distributed to stake holders (inclusive of both equity and debt stakes).

Income Statement: A financial statement showing the revenues, expenses, and income (the difference between revenues and expenses) of a company over some period of time.

Intermediary: One who is engaged to negotiate matters between two parties, and who for that purpose may be an agent, also called a Business Broker.

Letter of Intent (LOI): A preliminary outline of the major terms of a proposed transaction.

Leveraged Buy-Out (LBO): A transaction used for taking a public company private that is generally financed through the use of a high degree of debt collateralized by the company's assets.

Liquidity: The ease by which an asset can be converted to cash. For example, marketable securities are highly liquid assets, while real estate is not.

Market Value: See Fair Market Value.

Merger: The combination of two or more companies.

Merger Premium: The portion of a buy-out offer in excess of the Market Value of the target company immediately prior to the offer.

Net Income: A company's total revenues reduced by all of the costs of doing business, including depreciation, interest, taxes and other expenses.

Non-Compete Agreement: An agreement that prevents a party from engaging in competitive activities. Sometimes the buyer will request that the seller sign a non-compete agreement.

Non-Disclosure Agreement: An agreement that requires the signer to not divulge any stipulated information.

Non-Recurring Expenses: Refers to expenses that are not expected to be incurred in subsequent periods.

Payback Period: The length of time it takes to recover the initial cost of a project, without regard to the time value of money. For example, if a project costs $100 and brings in $20 per year, the payback period is 5 years.

Pledging Receivables: The act of using accounts receivable as collateral for a loan.

Privately-Held: A company whose stock is not traded on a public securities exchange.

Profit Margin: Determined by dividing Net Income by net sales and is expressed as a percentage. Profit margin is a measure of how efficiently the business is operating.

Public Company Comparable Analysis: A market-based valuation methodology in which the current share prices of similar publicly traded companies are analyzed. Derived ratios, such as Price to Sales, after adjustments, can be useful benchmarks in determining the value of a company.

Recast Financial Statements: The reconstruction of the past and current financial statements of a business to adjust for certain changes.

Retained Earnings: A capital account that measures a company's accounting earnings that are retained for reinvestment in its operations and not paid out as dividends.

Return on Equity (ROE): An indicator of profitability derived by dividing Net Income by Stockholders' Equity.

Return on Investment (ROI): A profitability measurement of an investment in a company, equal to the net income from the investment divided by the investment amount.

Selling Memorandum: The document that is prepared by a seller and its advisors that describes the business for sale including its history, products, markets, management, facilities, competition, financial statements, product literature, and a review of its prospects.

Small Business Administration (SBA): A federal agency that provides financial, technical and management assistance to help people start, run, and grow their businesses.

Small Business Investment Companies (SBIC): SBIC's are licensed and regulated by the SBA to provide funding for small businesses.

Term Sheet: See Letter of Intent.

Valuation: A comprehensive financial and operational review that focuses on pricing a business in anticipation of a sale or other reason.

Working Capital Management: The management of Current Assets and Current Liabilities to maximize short-term liquidity.

Bibliography

Raising Capital: How to Get the Money You Need to Grow Your Business Andrew J. Sherman / Hardcover / Kiplinger Books & Tapes / June 2000.

Valuation: Measuring and Managing the Value of Companies (3rd Edition) McKinsey & Company, Inc.,Jack Murrin,Tim Kroller,Tom Copeland,John Wiley,Tim Koller / Hardcover / Wiley, John & Sons, Incorporated / July 2000.

Mergers, Acquisitions, and Corporate Restructurings. Patrick A. Gaughan / Hardcover / Wiley, John & Sons, Incorporated / June 1999.

Mergers and Acquisitions: Managing the Transaction. Joseph C. Krallinger / Hardcover / McGraw-Hill Professional / March 1997.

Big Deal: Mergers and Acquisitions in the Digital Age. Bruce Wasserstein / Paperback / Warner / September 2001.

Buying Your Own Business. Russell Robb / Paperback / Adams Media Corporation / January 1997.

The Complete Guide to Mergers and Acquisitions: Process Tools to Support M&A Integration at Every Level. Timothy J. Galpin,Mark Herndon / Hardcover / Wiley, John & Sons, Incorporated / October 1999

Buyout: The Insider's Guide to Buying Your Own Company. Rick Rickertsen,Michael Lewis,Robert E. Gunther / Hardcover / AMACOM / March 2001

Harvard Business Review on Mergers and Acquisitions. Manufactured by Harvard Business School Press / Paperback / Harvard Business School Publishing / May 2001

Art of M&A Due Diligence. Alexandra Reed-Lajoux,Charles Elson,Charles Elson / Hardcover / McGraw-Hill Companies, The / May 2000

Mergers and Acquisitions Handbook for Small and Midsized Companies. Thomas L. West (Editor),With Jeff Jones / Hardcover / Wiley, John & Sons, Incorporated / March 1997

How to Join, Buy or Merge a Physician's Practice. Yvonne Mart Fox, Brett A. Levine / Paperback / Mosby-Year Book, Incorporated / August 1997

How to Buy a Great Business with No Cash Down. Arnold S. Goldstein / Paperback / Wiley, John & Sons, Incorporated / September 1991

Due Diligence Techniques and Analysis: Critical Questions for Business Decisions. Gordon Bing / Hardcover / Greenwood Publishing Group, Incorporated / August 1996

A Basic Guide for Buying and Selling a Company. Wilbur M. Yegge / Paperback / Wiley, John & Sons, Incorporated / October 1996

A Practical Guide to Acquisitions: How to Make a Success of the Most Risky Business Activity. Denzil Rankine / Paperback / Wiley, John & Sons, Incorporated / December 1997

Business Valuation Bluebook: How Successful Entrepreneurs Price, Sell and Trade Businesses. Chad Simmons / Paperback / Facts on Demand Press / May 2002

Financial Due Diligence: A Guide to Ensuring Successful Acquisitions. Stephen Bourne / Paperback / Financial Times/Prentice Hall / December 1999

Index

Accounting, 28, 94

Acquisition, 15, 19, 31, 32, 37, 38, 41, 42, 69, 70, 75, 76, 81, 92, 99, 102, 103, 104, 105, 108, 110, 112, 126, 127, 128, 140, 143, 144, 157, 158, 159, 160, 163, 168

acquisitions, 20, 48, 64, 98, 140, 149, 154, 156, 157, 158, 162

Addbacks, 86

Adjusted, 83, 84, 85, 86, 87

Adjustments, 94, 96

Advertising, 27, 43, 77

Agreement, 52, 57, 58, 146, 148, 165, 169

Amount, 101, 110, 114, 119, 160

Analysis, 76, 78, 114, 119, 151, 160, 161, 163, 164, 165, 167, 170, 175

Analyze, 65

Applying, 81, 83

Asking Price, 56, 108, 111

Assets, 56, 74, 90, 95, 96, 103, 110, 128, 166, 172

Assets-based, 104

Assumption, 15, 21, 62, 112

Auction, 164

Balance Sheet, 63, 95, 164

Bank, 52, 104

Borrow, 103, 104

Broker, 36, 37, 39, 41, 44, 59, 75, 93

Business, 3, 13, 14, 15, 17, 18, 19, 20, 21, 22, 23, 24, 25, 26, 29, 31, 32, 33, 34, 35, 36, 37, 38, 39, 40, 41, 42, 43, 44, 45, 46, 48, 49, 50, 51, 52, 53, 54, 56, 57, 58, 59, 60, 61, 62, 63, 64, 67, 68, 69, 70, 71, 72, 73, 75, 76, 78, 79, 81, 85, 86, 87, 88, 89, 90, 91, 92, 93, 98, 99, 100, 101, 102, 103, 104, 105, 106, 108, 109, 110, 111, 112, 113, 114, 116, 117, 119, 121, 123, 127, 128, 129, 130, 131, 132, 133, 134, 135, 136, 137, 138, 139, 140, 144, 149, 150, 151, 152, 153, 154, 155, 156,

157, 158, 159, 161, 162, 163, 164, 165, 166, 167, 168, 169, 170, 171, 172, 173, 174, 175

Business Brokers, 35, 39

Businesses, 39, 175

Buyer, 51, 55, 56, 57, 58, 59, 60, 61, 144, 145

Buying, 13, 17, 20, 21, 23, 131, 139, 145, 147, 148, 174, 175

Capital, 3, 96, 97, 121, 165, 166

Caribbean, 121

Cash, 63, 74, 95, 96, 97, 165, 167, 168, 175

Closing, 52, 53, 54, 59, 60, 93, 99, 100, 101, 104, 113, 116, 117, 126, 133, 144, 145, 146, 147, 154, 162

Closing Cost, 99

Collecting, 73, 122, 145

Commercial, 26, 165

Commissioned sales people, 134

Companies, 82, 172, 173, 174

Company, 47, 53, 64, 65, 66, 82, 109, 144, 145, 146, 147, 148, 149, 170, 173, 174, 175

Comparable, 165, 170

Competition, 68

Competitors, 77

Condition, 50

Contracts, 90, 92

Convenience, 26, 136

Cost, 76, 86, 94, 164, 166

Customers, 90, 136

Debt, 95, 160, 161, 163, 166

Deducted, 75

deposit, 52, 75, 100

Deposit, 52

Discounts, 137

Distribution, 26, 27, 66, 70, 77, 92, 134

Down payment, 56, 57, 58, 101, 102, 112, 113, 116, 117, 118, 121, 129, 154, 156, 161, 162

Down Payment, 58, 101, 160, 161

Due diligence, 33, 56, 63, 134, 167

Due Diligence, 49, 50, 56, 57, 58, 59, 60, 62, 63, 66, 67, 70, 129, 140, 149, 158, 167, 174, 175

Earnings, 85, 86, 87, 94, 96, 167, 171

Economic, 22, 23, 76, 154

Employee, 57, 74, 109, 132

Employees, 109, 131

Enterprise, 27

Equipment, 27, 47, 74, 95, 108, 110

Exclusivity, 92

Expansion, 78

Expenses, 53, 59, 81, 82, 86, 94, 110, 160, 170

Experience, 18

Facilities, 30, 159

finance, 23, 101, 103, 104, 106, 112, 121, 163

Finance, 26, 103, 114, 119

Finances, 133

Financials, 49, 63, 67, 83, 86, 108, 110, 160

Financing, 15, 20, 21, 35, 39, 51, 52, 54, 60, 62, 76, 97, 98, 104, 105, 108, 110, 111, 112, 121, 129, 133, 152, 156, 162, 165, 166

For down payment, 156

Franchises, 14

Frequency, 122

Funds, 154

Generating, 88

Good-faith, 75

Goodwill, 92, 95, 96

Group, 19, 20, 62, 121, 122, 123, 124, 175

Guarantee, 13, 14, 20, 22, 29, 45, 50, 71, 102, 105, 117

Handbook, 174

held, 73, 78, 80, 92, 144, 149, 154, 161

Hiring, 131

History, 64

Income, 36, 63, 74, 82, 85, 86, 88, 94, 96, 160, 161, 168, 169, 170, 171

Income Statement, 85, 168

Industries, 26

Industry, 18, 23, 24, 25, 26, 29, 31, 33, 34, 47, 63, 64, 67, 68, 70, 76, 79, 80, 83, 93, 136, 151, 158

Interest, 94, 96, 167

Internet, 27, 33, 35, 38, 39, 40, 70, 80, 83, 105, 149

Investigate, 67

Investing, 13, 22, 97

Investment Club, 62

Investors, 149

Issues, 127

Keeping, 22, 48, 122, 131, 136

Leads, 48

Lease, 52, 56, 59, 99, 110, 119

Lease-To-Own, 111, 116

Leasing, 28, 51, 56, 57, 58, 59, 60

Leasing Period, 58

Legal, 53, 54, 55, 59, 60, 62, 78, 127, 132

Letter of Intent, 38, 50, 51, 52, 53, 54, 55, 56, 57, 58, 59, 60, 61, 101, 129, 143, 168, 172

Leverage, 154, 168

Line of, 135, 147

List of, 24, 62, 73, 76, 150

Loan, 114, 119

Location, 36, 51, 108

Lower, 91, 101

M&A, 39, 174

Managing, 131, 133, 173

Market, 15, 65, 151, 153, 158, 160, 164, 167, 169

Marketing, 26, 43, 66

Member, 123, 124, 125, 157

Missing, 25, 89, 122

Multiple of, 73, 89

Multiples, 81

Net, 36, 82, 85, 86, 88, 94, 95, 96, 97, 160, 161, 164, 169, 170, 171

New Entrants, 65

New Owner, 51, 73, 77, 99, 100, 129, 130, 131, 135, 138, 139, 140

Newspapers, 27

Of assets, 128

Offer, 49

Operating, 23, 39, 57, 63, 74, 87, 100, 101, 105, 117, 134, 139, 140, 153, 154, 170

Operations, 94, 136

Opportunities, 34, 48

Option, 112, 116

Options, 96, 127

Owner Financing, 111, 112, 114, 116, 119

Owners, 41, 74, 78

Patents, 90, 92

Paying your, 134

Payment, 160, 161

Personal Residence, 113

Potential, 20, 29, 31, 34, 45, 65, 75, 77, 78, 79, 87, 89, 108, 117, 139, 140

Premium, 169

Price, 52, 58, 72, 110, 145, 160, 170, 175

Pricing, 137

Product Knowledge, 138

product or service, 68, 77, 137

Products, 26, 27, 28

Professional, 28, 91, 165, 173

Profile, 65, 108, 110

profit, 79, 85, 90, 139, 156, 164, 167

Profit, 74, 94, 170

Public, 80, 83, 154, 162, 168, 170

Purchase, 24, 32, 52, 56, 57, 58, 97, 128, 145, 160, 163

Raising Capital, 173

Rate, 25, 97, 165, 167

Ratio, 82, 83, 84, 85

Ratios, 166, 168

Real Estate, 110

Recast, 171

Receivables, 95, 96, 170

Refunded, 75

Regulations, 133

Rent, 79, 99, 135, 136

Researching, 29

Retail, 28, 36

Revenue, 36, 80, 82, 83, 94, 110, 160

Revenue Ruling, 80

Revenues, 86

Review, 54, 59, 64, 65, 157, 174

Salary, 81, 83, 86

Sales, 65, 66, 69, 86, 170

SBA, 105, 150, 171, 172

Search, 32, 158

Security Deposits, 102

Seller, 18, 32, 40, 41, 45, 52, 54, 55, 56, 57, 58, 59, 60, 62, 63, 65, 69, 73, 87, 89, 92, 93, 101, 102, 106, 111, 112, 113, 116, 117, 129, 131, 144, 146, 154, 167, 169, 171

Serious, 44

Service, 36, 47

Shareholders, 167

Software, 28, 90

Statistics, 23

Strategy, 23, 66, 68, 121

Suppliers, 69

Tax, 79, 94, 127

Technology, 28, 77

The market, 14, 33, 34, 41, 60, 76, 151, 162

The right business, 32, 40

Training, 26, 30, 60, 159

Transaction, 19, 20, 28, 42, 53, 54, 59, 60, 62, 87, 93, 98, 99, 109, 111, 112, 116, 127, 129, 144, 156, 163, 165, 166, 168, 173

Transfer, 56, 100

Utility, 99, 102

valuation, 72, 73, 76, 78, 80, 89, 90, 92, 149, 165, 167, 170

Valuation, 72, 73, 76, 78, 80, 89, 90, 92, 149, 165, 167, 170

Valuation Analysis, 38, 63, 67, 72, 85, 158

Venture Capital, 104, 106, 110, 153

Web Sites, 39

working, 14, 42, 44, 52, 100, 101, 104, 118, 154, 161

Working Capital, 100, 172

Yahoo!Finance, 80, 83

Sign-up For The Publisher's Free Online Course

Stay informed by signing up for our free online course to all Book/eBooks purchasers. In this virtual classroom you will have access to all the information included in the Book, updated chapters, information not included in the Book, **plus** the following:

- Introduction to sellers who prefer to receive long-term monthly payouts instead of a down payment and smaller monthly payments

- Eligibility to receive financing from our investment fund when you purchase your business. This is a private investment fund that invests solely in businesses purchased by those who have read the Book/eBook and signed-up to review the additional online material

- Unlimited e-mail consultation about businesses that you are looking to buy

- Lifetime membership to the web site and all its content

- Constantly updated information posted online to supplement your Book/eBook

- Free online forums and chats with industry experts

- A wealth of free resources from our online library (Course Documents section), including transaction documents, Due Diligence checklists, Valuation spreadsheets and no-money down strategies (all of which also included in the appendix of the Book/eBook)

To sign-up, e-mail us at info@rgllearning.com and include the following information:

- First and Last Name

- Email address (so we can contact you)

- A copy of the confirmation receipt from the web retailer that sold the book or eBook

Once we receive this information, we will send you your user id, password and domain name information, which will give you lifetime access to the online course and all the information on the web site.

Printed in the United States
1286400001B/226-246